++++++++++++++

Planning
for Protestantism
in
Urban America

++++++++++++++

Planning
for Protestantism
in
Urban America

+++

LYLE E. SCHALLER

ABINGDON PRESS • NEW YORK • NASHVILLE

PLANNING FOR PROTESTANTISM IN URBAN AMERICA

Copyright © 1965 by Abingdon Press

Standard Book Number: 687-31611-1

Library of Congress Catalog Card Number: 65-10812

Portions of this book are based on material which first appeared in pamphlets and periodicals. Acknowledgment is made to the following publications:
To *The Baptist Leader* for "The Local Church and Institutional Blight" (August, 1963)
To *The Christian Advocate* for "Public Housing: The Forgotten Frontier" (November 22, 1962), and "Must Every Church Be Self-Supporting?" (November 21, 1963)
To *Church Management* for "Integration" (January, 1962), and "The Storefront" (March, 1963)
To *The City Church* for "Public Policy Affects Church Planning" (September-October, 1961)
To *The Lutheran* for "To Relocate, to Merge, or to Dissolve" (August 8, 1962), "Expressways and Church Planning" (May 22, 1963), and "Some Congregations Spend Too Much" (July 15, 1964)
To *The Methodist Story* for "Beware the Numbers Game!" (February, 1964)
To *The Pulpit* for "The Dilemma of the Inner-City Pastor" (February, 1962) Copyright 1962 by Christian Century Foundation. Reprinted by permission from *The Pulpit*
To *This Day* published by Concordia Publishing House for "Lessons in Integration" (January, 1964)
To the Council of Southwestern Theological Schools, Inc. for "Planning for Protestantism" from *Church Planning*

SET UP, PRINTED, AND BOUND BY THE
PARTHENON PRESS, AT NASHVILLE,
TENNESSEE, UNITED STATES OF AMERICA

To Agnes

++++++++++++++++

Preface

✦✦✦✦✦✦✦

TODAY IN URBAN AMERICA PROTESTANT CHURCHES ARE continually involved in a struggle to maintain their integrity and relevance. The pressures of a highly mobile urban society are causing many churches to be more concerned with saving their own institutional life than with being faithful to their purpose. All too frequently the members recognize and respond to the secular forces of the world more readily than to the biblical imperative to bring the message of Jesus Christ to all men.

These stresses and strains can be seen most clearly as the leaders of the church meet to decide questions which will influence the future of the church.

How can the urban church plan effectively for the future, on the one hand, recognizing the impact of the changes which are occurring all around, and on the other hand, remembering that the church is not just another man-made institution, but rather is a part of the body of Christ? How can the urban church be faithful to its call, relevant to the life of the city, and responsive to the forces which are shaping its future? How can the church of today effectively plan for tomorrow's mission?

An answer to this question can be developed only if appropriate consideration is given to four important factors. The first of these is commitment to Christ as Savior and Lord. Without this commitment the church is only another institution, and the members are more likely to be concerned with preserving the institution than with serving Christ. Thus the primary commitment of the persons involved in church planning must be to Christ and to the mission of his church rather than to the contemporary institutional expression of the church. This may appear to be a perfectly obvious affirmation; however, failure to recognize the proper priorities of commitment is the most serious single obstacle encountered in the process of planning for the future of American Protestantism.

The second crucial ingredient in the effective church planning process is an understanding of the biblical nature of the church. This again should be obvious to everyone; however, so many American churchmen are much better acquainted with the institutional forms of the church than they are with the Acts of the Apostles or the book of Romans that this merits special emphasis. The decisive form of the New Testament church is one of servanthood. Wherever it is present the church must be prepared to fulfill its role as servant, and all efforts at church planning can be effective only if conceived within the context of servanthood.

The third essential factor in planning for the future of the Protestant churches in urban America is an affirmative acceptance of the role and importance of the institutional forms of the church. Institutional expressions of the church are legitimate orders of creation. They are essential if the church is to be an effective servant in a society in which institutions are growing in importance. New institutional forms of the church are needed if Christians expect to confront urban man with the gospel at all times and in all places. This acceptance of the institutional church must be tempered with the realization that new institutions should be created and old ones perpetuated only in response to genuine needs and to a sense of mission.

The fourth element in effective church planning is a sophisticated understanding of the dynamics of the planning process. Traditionally the major emphasis in planning has been to produce a single solution to a problem; sometimes the answer is presented in the form of a "master plan," sometimes in the form of a recommended specific course of action, sometimes as a series of alternatives.

More recently planners have recognized that planning is most effective when it is thought of as a continuing *process* in which everyone who will have a voice as a decision maker has the opportunity for participation. Thus it is the process, not the program produced by that process, which is of prime importance. This is especially true in American Protestantism where a consensus is so essential to effective decision making.

It is from this perspective that this book has been written. The bulk of the content is concerned with the planning for the church in its institutional forms, but this is predicated on the assumption that the forms are means by which the end goal of servanthood can be achieved.

The first chapter describes, through a case study approach, how a local church can use the planning process to rediscover its purpose and mission and to cope with some of the problems which challenge a church in contemporary urban

America. Many of the decisions made by a local church or a denomination will be influenced by external forces which range from the actions of governmental agencies to changes in the characteristics of the population. The impact of these external forces are described in the first two chapters.

The church is both an institution and a vehicle for the expression of God's love for man. The temptation for the churchman concerned with planning for the future of his church is to emphasize the sociological form of the institution; in recent years, however, theologians have contributed much to a richer understanding of the possibilities of planning. The nature and response to these contributions constitutes the theme of Chapter 3.

The current expressions of Protestant church planning trace their origins to comity and other efforts at inter-denominational cooperation. The fourth chapter is devoted to a critical analysis of this evolutionary process. One of the results of these various efforts at denominational and inter-denominational planning has been the accumulation of a rather sizable collection of surveys, reports, and case studies. From this collection of material, plus my own experiences, an attempt has been made to develop a series of guidelines which can be used by churchmen in the planning process. These principles and yardsticks are presented in Chapters 5 and 6.

During the past several years an increasing amount of concern has been expressed for the church in the inner city and the difficulties it faces there. The special considerations involved in planning for the church in the inner city are analyzed in Chapter 7. Two church-planning problems—urban renewal and racial integration—both of which began as inner city issues, but which have outgrown their original geographical limitations, are discussed in Chapters 8 and 9.

Someone once said that the most common role of the

planner is that he is the person who is called in at the last minute to share the blame. It would be unwise for me to comment on that definition; however, the second most frequent demand on the church planner is the request that he predict the future. The most presumptuous chapter in what may be labeled a highly presumptuous book is Chapter 10 in which an attempt is made to project certain trends and forces and to interpret the impact of these on the church of tomorrow.

It would not have been possible to write this book without the active cooperation of many people. High on this list are the more than one thousand clergymen from some thirty denominations who have been most generous in sharing their insights, experiences, observations, and reflections in individual interviews. Opportunities to share in planning meetings with individual congregations and with denominational committees also have been very rewarding and enlightening. In many respects this book represents a synthesis of my experiences with community planners and with dedicated churchmen (many friends fit into both categories). They are too numerous to name here, but their contributions cannot go unacknowledged.

Portions of this book are based on articles which have appeared in *The Pulpit, The City Church, The Lutheran, The Christian Advocate, The Baptist Leader, Church Management, This Day,* and *The Methodist Story.* A portion of Chapter 5 also appeared in the pamphlet *Church Planning* edited by Marvin T. Judy and published by Southern Methodist University Press. I am in debt to the editors of these publications for permission to reprint portions of these articles. Their encouragement and cooperation is gratefully acknowledged.

Finally a word of appreciation is due the trustees of the Regional Church Planning Office for the opportunity they

provided me to study the urban church, to marvel at the
workings of the Holy Spirit through the church, to share in
a variety of church planning experiences, and to restore my
confidence in the church as we see it expressed in its institutional forms.

—LYLE E. SCHALLER

Contents

✚✚✚✚✚✚✚✚

1

The Planning Process
✦✦✦

THE OFFICIAL BOARD OF ST. LUKE'S WAS DISCUSSING THE future of the church. Organized in 1902, the congregation had met for nearly twenty years in a frame building located on a residential street in a prosperous middle-class neighborhood in the city of Glendale. The congregation had grown consistently in those early years, and at the end of World War I the old building had been razed and a new brick "Akron Plan" structure erected on the same site. By 1930 the membership had passed the 700 mark.

The congregation had been fortunate in getting their mortgage paid off before the depression. Despite the economic squeeze, life for St. Luke's was comparatively simple until 1947, when some of the residents of the neighborhood began to move out to new homes in areas which were being annexed to the city.

The trickle soon turned into a flood, and by 1958 the characteristics of the population and the neighborhood around the church had changed substantially. Nearly two thirds of the residents were renters. Some of the larger houses, which had been remodeled during World War II to provide an apartment on the second or third floor, were being subdivided again, and now were occupied by three or four families. Forty years ago only a few houses were occupied by more than one family. Now only one third remained as single-family structures.

The first newcomers to the neighborhood after the war had appeared to be little different from the old residents. They were a little younger perhaps and had more modest incomes, but most of them had been born and reared in Glendale. By 1956 it became obvious that an increasingly large share of the people moving into the neighborhood had been born and reared in rural America, many of them coming from the farms of Illinois, Indiana, and Ohio. The majority, however, came from the coal fields of Pennsylvania and West Virginia or the hills of Appalachia. The first Negro did not move in until early last year, and now Negroes constitute nearly 15 per cent of the population.

These changes in the neighborhood had affected the composition of the membership at St. Luke's. The membership total was now down to 400; most of them were either long-time members or the children of old members. Less than one fourth were under forty years of age, and a majority had already celebrated their fifty-fifth birthday. Less than a hundred of the members still lived within a mile of the church, and many of these were too old to walk even that far.

Two of St. Luke's neighboring churches had sold their properties and followed their members to new homes on the periphery of the city. Both had shown a substantial increase in membership since moving into their new, modern plants.

One of the two old church buildings had been purchased by a Pentecostal congregation, the other by an independent Baptist group.

The possibility of relocation had been discussed repeatedly at St. Luke's, but the members could never agree on a specific course of action. The situation changed abruptly last week, however, when it had been announced that the right-of-way for the new expressway would come right up to the rear lot line of the church's property. Upon hearing this news the board was ready to listen carefully to ideas about the future of the church.

"This building was obsolete the day it was completed; American Protestantism had pretty much abandoned the Akron Plan by 1910," said the first speaker, a fifty-year-old architect and the son of a charter member of St. Luke's. "The cost of remodeling the present structure is not economically feasible. The smart thing would be to buy a new site out on the north side of the city, sell this for whatever we can get for it, and build a new, modern plant on an adequate-size site in a growing area."

"I wonder if we can afford to go and build a new church all by ourselves," asked the treasurer of the church. She was one of the pillars of the church and had been treasurer since 1951. "Our membership is half what it used to be; last year our receipts totaled 23,000 dollars, and we were able to end the year in the black only because we didn't pay the full asking on benevolences. I doubt if we can afford to move. My sister is a member at the Fairwood church; I wonder if we might merge with them? A lot of our members live out that way."

"The religious census taken last year by the Council of Churches indicated that one of the largest concentrations of unchurched people in all Glendale is located right in this neighborhood," stated a young man who had joined the church only three years ago. Fifteen years earlier, while both were in college, he had married the daughter of one of the trustees. After moving around the country for a dozen years he had been transferred to Glendale, and on the basis of family ties they had decided to make St. Luke's their church. "I think we should plan to stay here, perhaps remodel the building, and undertake a vigorous evangelism program to reach these people with the gospel of Jesus Christ. We might begin by trying to contact the people in the public housing project down the street."

As the evening wore on, the lack of a consensus became apparent to everyone. Finally the pastor suggested that they appoint a planning committee. A seven-member committee was appointed, and it was agreed that they would have three months in which to complete their report. With this decision the official board at St. Luke's took the first step in the planning process—a process which would help the entire membership in their effort to discover and fulfill their future role as a part of Christ's universal church.

Some of the members of the board expected that the planning committee would bring in a definitive answer to all their problems and they would one day be presented a pretty package which they could accept or reject. This was not the procedure that the planning committee chose to follow, however. The chairman of the committee, John Henderson, was a senior planner in the city's planning department, and he was hopeful that the goal of his committee would not be to produce an "answer" to the question of what St. Luke's should do. Rather, he hoped that the major contribution of his committee would be to help the congregation make an informed decision about its own future. The progress of Henderson's committee merits detailed consideration, for it illustrates the nature of the planning process as applied to decision making in Protestantism. It also provides some relevant illustrations of the planning problems confronting the church in urban America.

The Beginning of the Process

At St. Luke's, as it must everywhere, the planning process began with a desire to "do something." At first this was an undisciplined desire which accomplished little except to force nearly everyone to take a stand in favor either of remodeling or of relocating. The decision to study and plan enabled the church to harness this desire to "do something" and to divert it via the planning process into creative channels out of which appropriate constructive proposals could emerge.

An important part of the first step taken that night at the board meeting at St. Luke's was the admission that the church had a problem. While there may have been a difference of opinion over the exact nature of the problem, there was agreement that a problem existed, and there was a desire to solve it. This is the crucial first step in planning—to admit that something needs to be done and to be willing to do it. If these two elements are absent it is nonsense to talk about doing any effective planning. This does not mean that planning can occur only in the face of a crisis, but rather it means that people must recognize that past programs *may* not be adequate for future needs.

The planning committee, a seven-member group which was broadly representative of the congregation, sat down together at their initial meeting and decided that the first thing to do, as stated in the charge from the official board, was to decide what the real problem was. Very quickly it became apparent that they faced a threefold task. They could not define their problems without first agreeing on what was the purpose of their church. Was it to serve the scattered membership? Was it to serve the people living near the building? Was it to serve only interested persons of their own denomination? The members of the committee agreed that they could not state the purpose of St. Luke's nor formulate any goals without first knowing more about both the members of the congregation and the neighborhood.

In this meeting the St. Luke's group discussed three completely different steps in the planning process—definition of problem, formulation of goals (purpose of the church in this case), and data gathering. Their experience also illustrates how the various steps are intermingled and how many parts of the process may be carried on concurrently. Occasionally it happens that even the desire to plan and to take systematic action is not aroused until certain other steps, which are a part of the total process, have been taken. For example, in one congregation none of the members realized their church was not reaching the nearby residents until after members of the youth fellowship had made spot maps showing the residence of each member and Sunday-school pupil as a part of a district youth project. When the youth counselor brought this into a meeting of the evangelism committee it marked the beginning of a new era for that church.

The planning committee of St. Luke's, feeling the pressure of time, decided that they would form three subcommittees, inviting other members of the congregation to serve on each one. The first was assigned the task of gathering and analyzing all the relevant data they could bring together. The members armed themselves with copies of the self-study manual published by their denomination and began to systematically gather data on population trends, land-use patterns, location of church members, and other statistics. They interviewed the pastors of all the churches they thought might be reaching any of the residents of the neighborhood in which their church was located. They did this in an attempt to learn which churches were reaching the neighborhood residents and the type of ministry that was being rendered. They studied the program of their own church to determine who was being reached by the different elements and to uncover any weaknesses in the program. They compared the building facilities with the program and the apparent needs of the congregation and neighborhood residents. They asked themselves, "Is our program determined by the physical facilities of the church plant, by tradition and habit, by the wants of the congregation, or by the needs of the neighborhood?"

A second subcommittee concentrated its efforts on developing a general statement of the purpose of the church. They began by a careful study of the New Testament, seeking to discover what the Bible had to say to them about the reason for the church's existence. They kept asking themselves, "In the light of the New Testament what is the special role that God has for St. Luke's?" They felt constrained to justify the existence of St. Luke's at that place and time in history. As they studied, talked, and prayed certain goals for their church emerged from their deliberations. They began to prepare a tentative list of goals which they first discussed with other members of the larger planning committee and then with the congregation as a whole.

The third subcommittee tried to pinpoint the problems facing the congregation. At first one member suggested it was simply a matter of money. "If everyone would increase his pledge by 50 per cent, our problems would be solved."

Another said the major problem was the church's failure to reach teenagers and young adults.

Someone else said the problem was leadership. "It is almost impossible to get anyone to teach Sunday school or to work with the youth fellowship. That's why we're not reaching the children or the teenagers; we don't have the leaders."

Finally someone said that what was needed was a good

evangelism program. "That would solve all our problems. It would bring in more members, more money, and more teachers. Once this church starts to grow again we'll be able to attract more people. No one wants to come to a church that's going downhill."

By the time the meeting broke up everyone was feeling rather despondent. They had come to tackle what they thought was a simple assignment, to state the problem confronting St. Luke's. They went home feeling rather overwhelmed by the number and variety of the apparently insoluble problems facing their church. Each knew of other older churches that had reached the stage when they either closed their doors for good or merged with another struggling congregation. "Is St. Luke's about to die?" This was the question in the minds of several as they drove home after the meeting that evening.

All three subcommittees met regularly together to share their findings and ideas. They also made regular progress reports to the official board, and members of the subcommittees were given an opportunity to discuss their work at regular meetings of the various organizations within the church —the men's brotherhood, the different women's circles, the couples' club, the adult Sunday-school class and the Bible study groups.

As a result members of the congregation were not only kept informed on what was happening, but they also had the opportunity to contribute their own suggestions. Perhaps the most fruitful discussions were those which occurred when members of the three subcommittees came together. This was particularly helpful to the subcommittee charged with defining the problems of the church. They began to see that at their first meeting they had discussed only symptoms and not the real problem. Sometime later, when several men were standing around talking after church while waiting for their wives, one of the members of the goals subcommittee commented that their discussions had led him to see the purpose of the church as mission and that they were trying to formulate goals which would be consistent with such a definition of purpose. A member of the problems subcommittee overheard that remark and told his wife about it as they drove home together.

At the next meeting of his subcommittee he said, "Friends, I know what the problem of this church is. It isn't lack of money, or too few members, or lack of leadership. We've lost our sense of mission as a church."

Another responded, "You're right! I've been thinking about this, and it would be wrong for us to go out and ask people to join our church just because we need their time and money. We can never make any appeal to people unless we are concerned about them rather than about saving our church. Sometimes I think we're more concerned about being a club than being a church."

While there was considerable agreement with these comments, it was far from unanimous. "We still have to pay the preacher," said one. Another added, "You don't raise a 27,000-dollar annual budget just by being a do-gooder."

Despite the doubts and questions in the minds of a few, the planning committee decided they were ready to move into the next phase of the planning process—the drawing up of alternative courses of action.

Members of the planning committee had long been aware that a small but highly vocal group in the church wanted to sell the building and move to a new site on the periphery of the city. They also knew that most of the older members and several of the younger members wanted to stay. There was a third group which had seized upon the treasurer's suggestion of a merger with the Fairwood church, and a few had gone so far as to initiate conversations with Fairwood members on the subject.

Clearly St. Luke's was faced with three alternatives—to relocate, to stay, or to merge.

Merge, Relocate, or Remain?

By this time each member of the planning committee had strong inclinations toward one of the three possibilities. How could they objectively consider each alternative without letting their own opinions have an undue influence? Their efforts to answer this question required much more time than most church members are willing to give to such problems; however, the procedure they developed provided the members at St. Luke's with an unusual opportunity for informed decision making.

The planning committee scheduled three separate meetings on consecutive Tuesday evenings and invited all the members of the congregation to attend each one. In the letter sent to each family on the church's mailing list was a brief explanation of why a planning committee had been appointed and of some of the problems facing St. Luke's. The letter then went on to state that the possibility of relocation would be the subject for the first meeting; merger would be taken up at the second meeting; and the alternative of staying at the present site would be discussed on the third evening. They also enclosed on a separate sheet the statement of goals which had been developed by the committee. Basically this was the product of the subcommittee on purpose; however, it had been discussed by many groups within the church, and many suggestions had been incorporated into it.

In an effort to provide a relevant frame of reference for each meeting the planning committee had developed an agenda which called for each meeting to begin with fifteen minutes of Bible study in the book of Acts and with prayer.

This was to be followed by a brief statement by the chairman of the subcommittee on purpose who would suggest that the members evaluate the evening's presentation in terms of the statement of goals. Next was a twenty-minute general presentation by an outsider who had a special knowledge of the alternative that was the subject for the evening. He would be followed by a member of the planning committee who would present that alternative in positive terms, and the second hour would be devoted to questions and discussion.

For the first evening the committee was able to secure a professor from a nearby theological school who was just completing a study of church relocations. He began by telling of the experience of a church that moved from the central part of a large Midwestern city to a wealthy suburb.

Organized in 1843, the congregation had been at the same location for over a century when it began to consider moving in 1948. A number of neighboring main-line Protestant churches had either closed or relocated, despite an increase in the Protestant population—both white and Negro.

The membership roll had dropped in twenty years from 2,000 to 1,600. The forty-year-old building needed major repairs. Negroes were coming into the area south of the church, and an increasing number of members were moving to the suburbs. The church decided to stay, however, and a 75,000-dollar remodeling program was launched.

The decision was based as much on sentiment as on a sense of responsibility to the neighborhood. Before long some members reopened the question of relocation. A committee was appointed to study the situation and recommended to the congregation a move to the suburbs to better serve its membership. The plant was sold to a 3,700-member Negro congregation. A new site was purchased, and a 450,-000-dollar building program was launched on the basis that the new church would be "good for seventy-five to a hundred years."

The site selected turned out to be further from the center of the church and Sunday-school membership or the center of giving than the old site. It was within one-half mile of the center of the church's leadership, however, while the old location was four miles from that center. The old location was readily accessible by public transportation, but the new site was relatively inaccessible. The move was completed in 1954.

A decade later, within two miles of the site that was expected to be good for nearly a century, some notable changes were taking place as a result of the growing concentration of Jews and Negroes.

One main-line Protestant congregation has dissolved; another has its building for sale; a third is an integrated congregation with Negroes comprising three fourths of the membership; a fourth is on the verge of division over the question of integration; a fifth is well on the way to becoming a biracial church.

The professor then used the experience of this church to illustrate several characteristics often found in a congregation that decides to relocate.

1. Frequently the sentimental reluctance to abandon the old building is expressed in an initial decision to repair, remodel, or enlarge the existing plant. Sometimes this proposal is carried out; sometimes it is approved but never executed. In either case it seems to be a necessary preliminary step before the congregation is ready to sell out and start over at a new location.

2. The decision to relocate usually is supported by some rationalization that this is the "proper" path to a more effective ministry. The reasoning may be theologically un-

sophisticated, but apparently it is necessary for a congregation to assure itself that it is doing the right thing.

3. Regardless of how rapidly changes may have been occurring in the old neighborhood, the assumption is often made that the new site will be in the midst of great stability. In an age when the pace of change is accelerating this is both a naïve and a dangerous assumption.

4. Frequently the decision to relocate is not based on the needs of the neighborhood nor on the convenience of the membership, but rather on the desires of the leaders of the church.

5. The decision to relocate is usually influenced by the instinct for survival rather than by the imperative to serve. Many churches leave an area of high population density and relatively few churches to move into an area of low population density that is well supplied with main-line Protestant churches. Unquestionably there is an economic and social class orientation that is as significant as it is unscriptural.

When he had concluded his presentation there were only a couple of questions. Everyone was anxious to hear the details of the proposal to relocate St. Luke's.

The advocate of moving posted a large map which showed the location of St. Luke's, the homes of all resident members and of four sites which appeared to merit further consideration. After describing each location and the advantages, disadvantages, and prices of each parcel of property, he went on to develop a case for relocation without attempting to sell the group on a "specific" site.

After he concluded his presentation chairmen of the three subcommittees were asked to offer a brief reaction. This was followed by a very warm discussion which ran a half hour beyond the scheduled time of adjournment. As the members continued to discuss the idea of relocation it became apparent that many were opposed to this idea and that no one of the four proposed new sites had more than a handful of supporters.

At the second meeting the guest speaker was the regional executive of another denomination.

"Your planning committee invited me here to discuss in general terms what happens when two congregations decide to merge. It is my understanding that some of you feel that your church no longer has a mission in this neighborhood and that you may not have the strength nor the money necessary to relocate to a new site in a new neighborhood.

"During my twenty-five years as an executive in our denomination I have seen more than a score of churches come to the point at which you people here at St. Luke's find yourselves tonight. On the basis of these experiences I would like to take the liberty of expanding our subject for this meeting and to discuss not just merger, but rather two of the alternatives open to congregations such as this one. I would like to talk about both merger and dissolution. During the years I have spent as a minister I have had the opportunity to observe the funerals of a good many churches.

"For example just last year a sixty-year-old congregation in our denomination in a nearby city voted to dissolve. Their fifty-year-old building on an important intersection was in excellent condition. The congregation had reached its peak (543 members) twenty-five years ago. It was under a hundred when it closed.

"Negroes began to move into the area west of the church about ten years ago, but the neighborhood east of the church was still all-white when the church closed. Only a few of the members lived near the church, however, and the church did not have an effective program to reach the white residents, while no effort was made to reach the Negroes. The average age of the congregation's members was 63."

The guest speaker then went on to describe how this

case illustrates five factors characterizing churches that decide to dissolve.

1. Frequently the congregation is made up of older people who retain a sentimental tie to the church but lack the strength to carry on a vigorous evangelism program.

2. The church often is in a state of decline for so long that defeatism becomes part of its tradition.

3. Lack of an effective evangelism effort not only results in declining membership but also tends to perpetuate tired leadership.

4. Excessive delay in reacting positively to changes which occur in the neighborhood may make it impossible for the church to make the major adjustments necessary to survival.

5. When a large proportion of the membership lives outside the neighborhood the church is highly vulnerable. As long as a vigorous membership recruitment is in effect the church can thrive. It may even grow, and it can offer an attractive program as new members are funneled into leadership roles.

Once this cycle is broken it is extremely difficult to maintain the necessary vigor. The congregation becomes self-centered, and leaders begin to believe they have been elected for life terms. From then on the trend is almost irreversible. He concluded his remarks on dissolution by asking, "How long should such a church be allowed, or encouraged, to exist?"

"My answer," he said, "is that once death is inevitable, the denomination should step in and urge the dissolution of the congregation. While a struggling congregation may be an appropriate symbol for a minority religion, as Christianity always has been and still is, a dying church is a most inappropriate symbol for a religion founded on the concept of a living God."

When he had finished this portion of his presentation the

visitor asked if there were any questions. There were none. The members of St. Luke's were a little stunned by this blunt presentation. Each one sensed the parallel between the life and the death of the congregation he had used as an illustration and the recent trend at their church.

The speaker then moved on to talk about church mergers and began by pointing out that mergers are no longer as common as they were thirty or forty years ago. During the expansive boom of the 1920's there were many mergers in which two or three smaller congregations united in order to have the resources necessary for construction of a large building. During the 1930's the economic squeeze forced many congregations to merge in order to survive.

"Out of our experiences with mergers," he continued, "we have learned a few things that may help you here as you consider this alternative.

"Let me begin by telling you about a recent merger of two congregations that occurred here only a few years ago. Two churches of the same denomination needed new buildings. The older congregation had an excellent forty-year-old building in an area into which Negroes were moving. The 285-member congregation wanted to get out but did not feel strong enough to relocate.

"The younger congregation had outgrown its premises and wanted a new building. The older congregation sold its building for an amount equal to the sum the younger congregation had in its building fund. The two congregations merged and the new building was completed. But only 150 members from the older congregation went along."

From this example he pointed up two common generalizations that apply to mergers and might be relevant to the situation at St. Luke's and its possible merger with the Fairwood church.

1. Two and two equals three not four. The membership

for the new congregation normally is not equal to the sum of the two congregations, but to about 75 per cent of the combined total—or less. Merger provides some members with a convenient opportunity to drop out, particularly when the old building is being abandoned.

2. Two congregations can be merged psychologically and spiritually if they join on equal terms and are confronted by a common challenge. He pointed out that sometimes mergers do not work out well, however.

"For example, several years ago one of our churches, a 500-member German congregation, lost its church through fire. They began using the nearby church of a 300-member congregation of the same denomination. After prolonged discussion, during which time the pastor accepted a call to another church, the congregation voted to accept the invitation to merge with their smaller neighbor. The merger was encouraged by denominational officials.

"During the next fourteen years the merged congregation grew from 550 (in this case 500 plus 300 equaled 550) to nearly 700. Today the pastor says, 'I serve three congregations. The German, the English, and the people who have joined since 1948.' The church needs more space, though church attendance is not exceptional, if it is to provide an adequate ministry to its neighborhood. It is in desperate need of lay leadership and struggles to meet an inadequate budget.

"This situation illustrates that for churches, as for people, a marriage of convenience may be a marriage without love and may lead to a life of misery and despair rather than one of joy and service. Merger is not necessarily the synonym for unity."

Following this presentation there were several questions and the visitor referred to several large well-known local churches, which were the result of earlier mergers, as ex-

amples of how church mergers can be successful. He then
went on to make a point that stuck in the minds of most
of those present for a long time to come.

"My experience leads me to believe that you can predict
the probable outcome of a church merger. If two congregations come together because of a vision that unites them,
they can be very effective in carrying out the Lord's work
and fulfilling their mission. I believe they can look forward
to a rewarding and enriching experience. If they come together out of a sense of weakness, despair, and defeat, seeking primarily to postpone the final day of reckoning, I am
convinced that it will be very difficult for the new merged
congregation to carry on a fruitful ministry."

The next item on the agenda called for a presentation of
the merits and disadvantages of a possible merger of St.
Luke's and Fairwood. This was made by a panel consisting
of the treasurer and chairman of the official board of St.
Luke's and the chairman of the trustees of the Fairwood
congregation. It was obvious that none of the panel members had strong positive feelings toward the merger, and in
the subsequent discussion as much time was spent on relocation or dissolution as on merger. The visiting denominational executive suggested that few churches actually have
all three alternatives open as viable alternatives. If the congregation is seriously considering closing it almost certainly
is too weak to relocate. If it can realistically consider relocation it probably is too strong to justify dissolution. Merger
frequently is a compromise choice.

He concluded the evening by stating that, in his opinion,
congregations which are seriously considering the possibilities of relocation, merger, or closing frequently share three
common characteristics.

1. They have become irrelevant to their neighborhood.
This may be a result of changing land uses, such as the in-

flux of industry or the construction of freeways. Far more often it is because the congregation has lost interest in the neighborhood.

2. The congregation appears to have lost sight of the biblical concept of the church and replaced it with a strong proprietary interest in the church as a club.

3. The congregation has lost its sense and spirit of mission. Usually the evangelistic efforts are halted or inhibited because of class barriers. Race is the most obvious barrier to effective evangelism, but social and economic class considerations may be nearly as common, even if less conspicuous.

These were strong statements, and most of the members went home in a very troubled state of mind. Several wondered, Is St. Luke's a sick church?

The possibility of staying and attempting to serve the residents of the neighborhood was the subject for the third meeting. Their "consultant" for the evening was the pastor of an inner-city congregation of a different denomination located less than a mile from St. Luke's. One of the members of the subcommittee in charge of the self-study had met him when they were visiting the churches in the area and had suggested that this minister be invited to come over and discuss with them what is involved in a ministry to a changing neighborhood.

"How does a congregation go about serving the people who live within the shadow of the church spire, people the church thus far has not been able to reach?" With this question the visiting pastor began to share his experiences with the people at St. Luke's.

"Obviously this is not a simple challenge; if it were it would not be a problem. Perhaps the beginning point for an examination of this issue is in the challenge itself, Why is this a difficult task for inner-city churches but not for suburban churches? After this is understood it is possible to discuss the attributes of churches able to accept the challenge.

"This injunction to serve the neighborhood usually is offered on the premise that Protestantism should operate on the basis of a geographical parish. Each church should have a 'primary parish' made up of the people living within a mile or less of the building, and the needs of the residents of this area should be a major governing force in shaping the program of the local church.

"A large percentage of the churches in American Protestantism no longer can be described as geographical parishes, however. Today most churches serve a 'parish' which is delineated primarily on ethnic, cultural, or social class considerations rather than on geography. It is true that most new churches are organized on the premise that they will serve the residents of a specific geographical area, but it is also true that relatively few congregations which have passed their fifth birthday actually do relate primarily to a geographical parish.

"This is as true of many suburban, small-town, and rural churches as it is of old churches in the central city which have been left behind by the population migration to suburbia. Each usually serves people drawn from two or three strata of society. Rarely does the composition of the congregation match the characteristics of the population living in the neighborhood.

"While this condition has not produced crisis size problems for most suburban or small-town churches, it has caused many inner-city congregations to consider radical alternatives of action.

"Why hasn't it caused equally severe problems for the suburban churches?

"The answer is fairly obvious if one studies the census

reports showing the characteristics of the population in various communities. In most communities the church is confronted with a mobility rate which is about the same as that facing the church in the inner city. In most communities, however, the people who move in tend to have the same demographic characteristics as those who have moved out. As 'our kind of people' move out usually they are replaced by persons who also are our 'kind of people.' This has not been the case in inner-city neighborhoods such as surround both your church and my church. In terms of income, occupation, race, cultural heritage, ethnic characteristics, language, and education the newcomers frequently differ from those who have moved away. Thus churches such as yours and mine find it difficult to draw "replacement members" from the newcomers to the neighborhood. It is easier and less threatening to seek to maintain the loyalty of the members who have moved to the suburbs. This can be achieved most readily if nothing is changed, so that the non-resident member can return and find conditions pretty much as they always have been. In these churches Sunday becomes as much a day of homecoming as it is a day of worship.

"As time passes on, however, so do some of the old members; others move beyond commuting distance; and a few yield to the pressures, perhaps exerted by their children, to transfer to a church nearer their home.

"My church reached this stage a few years ago, and I understand that this is the present state of affairs at St. Luke's."

"That is precisely why we asked you to come to this meeting tonight," interrupted the chairman, "to tell us what happened at your church."

"It took our members several years to realize what was happening," responded the visitor, "and for some time the chief reaction was to work on the budget to keep expenditures down to the level of the church's income. Eventually some of the members began to suggest relocation. At this point the church council decided to invite one of the men from our national headquarters to come out and advise us on the matter of relocation.

"He spent three days with us and recommended that we postpone our discussions on relocation and give serious consideration to staying and serving the people in our neighborhood. It was at that time that the pastor of the church, who had been there for nineteen years, resigned to accept a call to another church. I was called to succeed him with the clear-cut understanding that the congregation was committed to a neighborhood-oriented ministry."

The minister then went on to describe some of the specific activities in which his church was engaged and some of their problems. Before long he was being interrupted repeatedly by questions. It was apparent that his story had captured the imagination of many people at St. Luke's.

During the course of the evening he made several points that appeared to be highly relevant for churches such as St. Luke's.

1. The decision to stay and serve the residents of the neighborhood means undertaking a new ministry while striving to continue the existing ministry to the present congregation. This is a very difficult task and can result in the creation of some very serious tensions. Some involve the pastor and the demands on his time.[1] Others involve the old nonresident members who "know how the church should be run" and the new members who have a firsthand acquaintance with the needs of the people in the neighborhood. Some tensions will develop over a struggle for leader-

[1] For an extended discussion of this very important point see the description of the dilemma of the inner-city pastor, pp. 157-61.

ship, others over financial issues, and still others over use of the building for neighborhood activities.

2. It may be that only the very strong or the very weak congregations are able to accept the challenge to shift to a neighborhood-oriented ministry. The strong can do this because they have the lay leadership, the staff, and the finances necessary to minister to the old congregation and to help them achieve a large sense of mission, and also to reach out and develop a new congregation with indigenous leadership from the neighborhood. They have the strength and the resources to overcome the resulting tensions which split a weaker congregation.

The very weak congregation also may be able to make this shift, but for quite different reasons. In their case the weakness of the congregation usually involves financial assistance from the denomination. This means that part of the decision-making process is shifted to a point outside the local church, and thus many of the tensions which might otherwise develop are avoided. The denominational offer of financial assistance may be predicated on the congregation's willingness to make an all-out effort at ministering to nearby residents.

By contrast those inner-city congregations which have a moderate degree of strength frequently are too strong to secure denominational assistance and too weak to unilaterally finance additional staff. They still have enough evidence of vitality to encourage those who believe that the church can survive without undertaking a strong evangelistic program aimed at neighborhood residents. Others will perceive that any radical shift in the orientation of the program will result in disruptive and unpleasant tensions, because both the proponents and opponents of any such change have vigorous leaders. The pressures to maintain the status quo counter the pressures of the biblical imperative to serve, and a stalemate results. This sometimes takes the form of a self-study program which never reaches the implementation stage. In many such congregations the sense of mission gets through to some of the members, but the conservative leadership has enough strength to successfully propose a building program or a remodeling project which captures this desire to "do something" and diverts it to a safe and harmless course.

3. Experience suggests that occasionally the goal of reaching the people in the neighborhood of a church made up of nonresident members can best be accomplished by dissolving the congregation, turning the asserts over to the denomination, and helping the old members find new church homes. When this painful process has been completed the denomination calls a new minister (it must be a new man; if the former pastor stays some of the old members will return), finances a fresh start, and undertakes a vigorous new program directed toward the religious needs of the nearby residents. Several of today's most successful inner-city operations are a result of this type of denominational action. It is expensive—usually an annual subsidy of 15,000 to 30,000 dollars is required—but it avoids all the problems and tensions which are involved in trying to transform an old nonresident congregation.

This alternative also has several disadvantages. It eliminates the opportunity for members of the old congregation to experience the thrill of recognizing and fulfilling a sense of mission. It is a heavy drain on the denominational treasury. It may cause many of the old members to resent the "dictatorial methods" of the denominational officials involved. There is the ever-present danger that the new church will soon become a congregation drawn largely from one social class grouping rather than from all the nearby residents. Sometimes the old building is not really an asset and is completely inadequate for the new neighborhood-oriented program. When one sums up the advantages and disadvantages of each alternative, however, this frequently, but not always, will be the most logical choice.

By the time they had completed this series of meetings the members of St. Luke's had learned a lot about the problems confronting the urban church today. They also had made significant advances in the planning process.

They had recognized the problems confronting the church. They had developed a set of goals which were consistent with the biblical concept of the church and which had been accepted by the members as the guideposts for action decisions. They had explored in depth several alternatives open to the church. In this latter stage they had sharpened the definition of their goals, discovered new problems, and added to the list of questions which needed answering. They had also been able to involve a relatively large number of members in this entire learning and sharing experience.

Some also discovered that the planning process involves the interaction of many different steps and stages. One member of the planning committee noted this in a remark he made to the chairman. "You're always talking about moving on to the next stage of the planning process, but it seems to me that we never leave any of the other steps behind us. We don't really move on, we actually just add another dimension to our thinking and our approach to this whole issue."

"That's not a bad way to describe this whole process," replied the chairman in an agreeable tone, "and now let's open up another dimension. Next we'll ask the self-study committee to give a detailed report to the entire congregation. On the basis of their work they were the ones who suggested that our basic alternatives were to relocate, merge, or stay and undertake a new ministry to the neighborhood. Perhaps their report will help the congregation choose a specific course of action."

It should be noted here that while St. Luke's resembles the typical urban church in many respects, the alternatives open to it are not the only ones that might grow out of a systematic approach to planning for the future. In other congregations the alternatives might be centered on changes in program, on broadening the scope of the church's ministry, on new possibilities for the creative involvement of the laity, on building problems, or on the congregation's relationships to other churches.

One of the reasons why the planning process of St. Luke's stressed the institutional nature of the church was that certain external institutional pressures were changing the physical environment in which the church is located. The three major institutional pressures on St. Luke's were (1) the nature of and condition of their physical plant, (2) the public housing project which was opened three blocks away in 1958, and (3) the proposed expressway with the edge of the right-of-way at the church's rear lot line. None of these are unusual conditions in urban America today. St. Luke's dilemma was unusual only in that all three conditions were present. All three were matters to which the self-study subcommittee had devoted considerable study.

What Is an Asset?

The chairman of the self-study subcommittee, an accountant, opened the next meeting by saying: "I was asked to chair a self-study committee, but as time passed I decided that a more appropriate title would be the 'Balance Sheet Committee.' Our primary concern seemed to be to discover what are the assets and the liabilities of our church.

"We won't have time to give a complete report tonight

because we want to concentrate on only three subjects. To give you an idea of what we have been doing, however, we have prepared a mimeographed report here which should help you decide on where we should go from here. You'll notice that the summary sheet is prepared in the form of a balance sheet, and we have attempted to list what we consider to be the major assets and liabilities of our church.

"For example under assets we have listed such items as no debt, farsighted pastoral leadership, a friendly congregational atmosphere, the interest and support of a major denomination, and the power of the Holy Spirit. Under liabilities we have such diverse items as an obsolete building, a poor level of giving, the low percentage of young, new members and the high proportion of elderly persons—don't misunderstand me now on that, it's not the older people who are a liability, most of the pillars of this church are in that category, rather it is the *high proportion* of older members that is the liability.

"We haven't completed our work yet because we haven't been able to decide on all the liabilities and assets. For example, we have nearly thirty-three members living in that new subdivision west of the golf course. Are they a liability or an asset? If we decide to relocate on the Jackson property they are an asset, since all are within walking distance of that site. If we decide to stay here and concentrate on reaching the people in this neighborhood, however, we should perhaps consider those thirty-three members a liability because the closest one lives nearly six miles from here.

"I don't want to argue that particular point now, but it does relate to what I do want to talk about with you.

"What is an asset?

"Take our church here. If we try to sell it we'll be lucky to get 40,000 dollars for the land and building. If we stay we'll have to put 100,000 dollars into remodeling and providing off-street parking. If we relocate that means buying land and erecting a building. It will cost us at least 200,000 dollars—maybe 300,000 dollars—to duplicate the space we have here. I ask you, is our building an asset worth 40,000 dollars or 200,000 dollars? Or is it a liability?

"It seems to me that the only way we can decide what our assets really are is to define our purpose in pretty specific terms and then to evaluate our resources against that purpose.

"One more example may help you see what I mean. Three blocks away is Riverside Terrace, a public housing project for over 800 families. We have only one member in the whole project, and the pastor tells me two other families look upon St. Luke's as their church.

"If our purpose is to get more members in order to increase the budget the project is no asset. If our purpose is to reach people with the good news of Jesus Christ, however, maybe Riverside Terrace is an asset which we have ignored for too long.

"We all need to spend a little more time considering this question of what are the real assets of this congregation.

"We also must spend some time this evening discussing in detail the probable impact of certain external forces on our future—including our responsibility to the residents of Riverside Terrace and the possible impact of the new expressway in our backyard."

After nearly an hour's discussion on the substance of these two external forces the group moved on to an analysis of alternative courses of action. This was the third and concluding item on the evening's agenda and perhaps the most fruitful.

As happens so often when each possibility is examined in detail, the alternatives have a way of sorting themselves out. Every person who had attended each of the four general meetings was thoroughly convinced that St. Luke's must stay and serve the residents living near the church. Some members had held this view for months; others became convinced rather recently.

The Climax of the Planning Process

Without ever thinking of it in these terms, the people at St. Luke's had informally taken the next step in the planning process. They had elected a specific course of action from among several alternatives.

Before the meeting adjourned the planning committee was asked to prepare a detailed program showing how St. Luke's might implement the decision to stay and serve its neighborhood.

Six weeks later at a congregational meeting the planning committee formally presented its recommendation that St. Luke's should undertake a major effort to minister to the residents of the neighborhood. This was unanimously approved after less than fifteen minutes' discussion. Most of the questions concerned the new expressway. When it was explained that in this neighborhood the highway would be depressed about twenty feet below grade and that, therefore, the anticipated problems of noise and esthetic considerations would be minimized, the last objectors withdrew their reservations and spoke in support of the motion.

Next the planning committee recommended adoption of a detailed six-point action program. This had been adopted by the official board at its last meeting and also had been explained in a carefully prepared pamphlet which had been mailed to each family about ten days after the board meeting. Earlier copies of all reports, including the final report on goals, had been distributed to all members.

Two of the recommendations were concerned with the remodeling program and the acquisition of land for off-street parking. A third called for an every-member canvass under the direction of one of the professional fund raisers from the national headquarters of the denomination. The other three concerned programs and merit more consideration here.

1. Every member of the church should be asked to share in an evangelism program which would be limited to the homes located within one-half mile of the church. The calls would be made on the premise that the members were interested in the people living in the vicinity of the church. The people visited would be invited to share in those parts of the church's program which appealed to them, but the primary purpose of the call would be to build bridges of Christian friendship between the visitor and the visited, bridges which would have as their foundations a Christian's love and concern for his fellow man.

2. The program of the church would be revised with an emphasis toward a more meaningful ministry to the nearby residents. This detailed recommendation included creation of a weekday nursery school, an after-school program for junior-high youngsters, a golden age club, Bible study groups which would meet in the homes, and a 5:00 P.M. Sunday worship service for those who had to work Sunday mornings. It also recommended cooperation with the neighborhood conservation council that had just been organized by a field worker from the city's urban renewal department.

3. An associate minister should be sought—contingent upon the success of the every member canvass—who would have as his primary duty the responsibility of developing a pastoral relationship with the residents of Riverside Terrace. This second minister was to be a part of the fellowship at St. Luke's, and it was hoped that he could help others develop a meaningful relationship to St. Luke's. It was to be clearly understood, however, that his ministry to the residents of

Riverside Terrace should not be restricted by institutional concepts of the form of Christ's holy church.

After this six-point program had been approved by the congregation it became the church's "master plan." It not only was a course of action, but also became an important reference point for all decisions on the administration and ministry of the church. The easiest portion of the program was that concerning property repair, acquisition, and remodeling. This was tackled first and with the greatest enthusiasm. It was a little harder to raise the additional funds for employment of an associate minister, but this was accomplished, and the pastor, his associate, and a few dedicated laymen began to enlarge and revitalize the program of the church. The hardest part of the entire "master plan" was the proposal for "person-to-person" calling.

Finally they recognized that effective planning must be continuous and must include adequate provisions for a systematic review of all steps including implementation. St. Luke's provided for the election of a "Committee to Review the Program," which was directed to report to the annual meeting on progress, new developments, and suggested changes. This is a good method, but a better one would provide for a continuing process of review, perhaps through the official board. In fact, this is what often does happen, and at St. Luke's there was a healthy process of review throughout all the early stages of the process. All elements in the entire program—purpose, goals, descriptive data, program, results, and plans—should be subjected to continuous scrutiny. Conditions do change, and a successful program may alter the goals just as changing conditions may alter the needs. An effective review provision will help insure that the program is relevant to the contemporary needs.

This is an example of how the planning process may work in practice. The same steps apply to use of the process by a local church, a city government, a denomination, a private business, or an interdenominational agency.

Planning can be most helpful if one first thinks of it as a continuous and dynamic process rather than simply as a product which can be handed out in package form. The second consideration to keep in mind in effective church planning is the need to tie the planning process in closely with the point at which decisions are made. The system of church government and the size of the congregation at St. Luke's made this rather easy, but in larger congregations this is a more difficult problem, for there are many different points where important decisions are made. It is essential that each of these decision-making points be involved in the continuing planning process.

Finally, the experience of St. Luke's provides an instructive case study because it illustrates how external forces, such as highways and public housing, can affect the life and ministry of the local church. In today's urban society these external forces are so significant that they merit detailed consideration by anyone concerned with contemporary church planning.

2

External Forces on Church Planning
+++

TRADITIONALLY MANY AMERICAN PROTESTANTS HAVE AT-
tempted to keep the church pure by isolating it from much
of the mainstream of life. "Keep the church out of politics
and politics out of the church" is an injunction which has
been heard many times. Similarly many churchmen believe
that the clergy should concern themselves only with "spiritual" issues and ignore contemporary problems on race and
economic and social issues. Unfortunately this type of thinking has influenced church planning. All too often a local
church or a denomination develops a course of action without giving adequate consideration to important secular
forces which affect the life and ministry of the church. Two
of the most important of these are the actions of various governmental agencies and basic population trends, and an
analysis of these two will illustrate the necessity of considering external forces on the life and ministry of the church.

The Impact of Government

For more than two decades Protestantism has been busy reacting to the major demographic trends—the migration from rural to urban America and the growth of suburbia. Both of these trends were greatly influenced by decisions made by the federal government. A more detailed examination of these two developments will demonstrate the impact of governmental actions on church planning.

The decline in the farm population has been going on for many years, but it is only during the past two decades that this has posed major problems for Protestant churches. Between 1910 and 1940 the percentage of the nation's population living on farms declined from 33 to 20 per cent. This did not, however, have any serious effect on the rural church, for the actual number of Americans living on farms decreased only slightly—from 32,000,000 in 1910 to 30,500,000 in 1940, or an average decline of only 50,000 persons per year. During the 1950-60 decade the farm population dropped to the 20,000,000 level, the lowest total in more than a hundred years. In one year—from April, 1956, to April, 1957—the population declined by 1,800,000, a greater decline than for the entire 1910-40 period. Full-time (thirty-five hours or more weekly) agricultural employment declined from over 6,000,000 in 1947 to 3,100,000 in 1962. Using the Census Bureau's new definition for "farm residents" the current farm population totals 14,000,000 persons, less than one twelfth of the nation's total population. It is no small wonder that the rural church is in trouble.

This decrease in farm population and the accompanying decline in rural America has largely been a result of the development *and practice* of improved production techniques. The federal government has been the key factor in both aspects of this change. From 1836, when the Patent

Office began to distribute plants and seeds to farmers, through the Morrill Act of 1862, which donated public lands for the support of agricultural colleges, through the establishment of experiment stations and the offering of financial support for the familiar county agent, the federal government has made a tremendous contribution to the science of farming. For decades, however, the maximum benefits to be derived from these scientific advancements were not realized. Tradition, fear of the effects of over-production (dramatically illustrated by the farm depression which followed World War I), and ignorance all played a part in this reluctance to take advantage of the latest ideas on farming. Many farmers were like the one who, when approached by his county agent with a proposal for improving the effectiveness of his operation, replied, "I'm not farming now half as well as I know how."

Implementation of these technological and scientific advances required new incentives and inducements. These were forthcoming during the 1938-41 period, largely as a result of actions taken by the federal government. From its earliest days agriculture had demanded large quantities of manual labor. Through the first thirty-five years of this century the typical farm relied on members of the family for most of the necessary labor and on the traditional hired man for the balance. The federal wage-and-hour act of 1938 threatened this pattern. While it did not apply directly to farm labor, it did set a new national standard that lured many members of the agricultural labor force to new fields of endeavor. Eventually this legislation priced unskilled labor out of the farm market.

Almost simultaneously the national defense effort created a new demand for manpower, both in the armed forces and in the civilian labor market. Within the space of about three years the situation had changed from one in which the farmer could secure an almost unlimited quantity of help at very low wages to one in which the farmer found hired help to be both scarce and expensive. He was forced to turn to mechanical labor-saving devices, despite any misgivings he may have had about the cost of such changes.

This conversion to new methods required a substantial capital investment. Naturally many farmers were reluctant to take such a risk unless there was an assured market and a guaranteed price level.

This was provided in general by World War II and in particular by the so-called Steagall Amendment to the 1941 congressional act which extended the life of the Commodity Credit Corporation. Quite simply it guaranteed the farmer that the government would provide a minimum price level for certain basic crops, regardless of the quantity produced, for the duration of the war plus two full calendar years following the termination of hostilities. In 1948, when the legislation was about to expire, it was extended for two years and provision made for a "permanent support program."

The net effect of this legislation by the federal government was to assure the farmer he could afford to make the financial investment necessary to take advantage of the latest technological developments. The price-support program guaranteed him a market for his produce and the income necessary to amortize his investment in machinery, fertilizer, and buildings. With this assurance the farmer mechanized his operation. The date of this change can be illustrated by various statistics—possibly the most significant of which is in 1945, when for the first time in history the number of tractors exceeded the number of horses and mules on American farms. The direct result has been a doubling of the per-acre yield in wheat, potatoes, corn, cotton, and other crops. One farmer can now grow the food for twenty-five persons—twice the productivity of his 1940 counterpart.

An indirect result of this agricultural revolution is that literally thousands of rural Protestant churches are in trouble. Their farm constituency has declined to the point where some churches have closed their doors and many more are faced with no other effective alternative. The small family farm, which made up the bulk of the membership of thousands of country and small-town churches, is now being replaced by the large corporation farm with relatively few employees per unit of land.

We are not yet to the end of this chapter, however. A paper prepared by Lauren K. Soth for President Eisenhower's Commission on National Goals pointed out that America probably could continue to increase farm production—even with a 50 per cent decline in farm labor. The commission suggested as a national goal the vocational relocation of 1,500,000 farm operators during the 1960's. While the commission suggested that it would be desirable to provide the new jobs locally, it is questionable whether this latter goal can be achieved.

Obviously the nation—and the church—has yet to feel the full effects of policies adopted by the federal government twenty years ago.

This exodus from the farm is only one of a series of factors that have provided new challenges for the urban church. For many years American cities have owed part of their growth and prosperity to a continual influx of people from rural areas. In earlier days these newcomers presented no problems. Frequently they were the more adventuresome, the more ambitious, the more adaptable members of the rural community or else they would not have left home. Furthermore the city needed them. There were places for the skilled and talented and also for those who could offer little more than a good pair of hands and a strong back. Both they and the cities thrived.

Today the situation is different. Many of those leaving the farm do so, not from choice, but from economic necessity. Frequently they continue to think of home as the place back in West Virginia or Kentucky from which they came. They return at every opportunity and are slow to become a part of the urban community. Many have no talents or skills to offer in the labor market. Many are Negroes, who encounter both cultural and racial barriers. At the same time, the city is different. Industry is hiring fewer and fewer unskilled workers. The demand for domestic help has almost disappeared. The city no longer welcomes the displaced farm family. Many of them are, in fact, unemployable.

These newcomers are moving into dwellings that were often occupied by old-line Protestant church members who have moved to the suburbs. Sometimes their church has moved with them; more often it has remained behind. Of the churches that decide not to move (only a few affirmatively decide to stay), some focus their attention on their old membership, many of whom now live far from the church. Others try to "serve their neighborhood" but find a major cultural barrier between themselves and the newcomers.

Many a pastor muses, "If only my old members had not moved to suburbia we would have the leadership and the financial support necessary to meet the challenge offered by these newcomers." Why have his members moved to suburbia? The reasons are many and varied but one of the most significant factors has been the housing policy of the federal government.

In the eighteen years following the end of World War II 17,000,000 one-family homes were built in this country, approximately one half of them with federal credit support. Most of these have been constructed either on the fringes of the nation's larger cities or in suburban communities. The nature of the FHA and VA requirements have made it easier to finance a new house than an old one.

In addition, the per-unit costs of arranging financing have been lower for large-scale developments than for individual homes. Finally, the low down payment and long-term mortgage policies of the FHA and VA have opened up the possibility of homeownership to two new categories of Americans. The first includes millions of families who did not have the large down payment required for conventional mortgages nor the credit to secure an uninsured mortgage. The second group includes those families, mostly younger ones, who because of occupational demands find it necessary to move frequently. The minimum equity feature plus the enlarged market resulting from the easier credit policies on housing have made it "cheaper to buy than to rent" for many couples. Here again the policies of the federal government have been significant. By permitting payments for property taxes and interest to be listed as deductible items in calculating a person's net income for tax purposes, the government has encouraged homeownership and discouraged renting. Thus a person buying a home with a 15,000-dollar mortgage may find his 150 dollar monthly payments are actually costing him only 85 to 90 dollars, and his depreciation and maintenance costs are offset by inflation. (Rental of a similar house probably would cost him 125 to 150 dollars monthly with no income tax advantages.) Thus a natural postwar demand for single-family housing has been greatly increased. Much of this demand has been met by converting thousands of acres of vacant land on the outskirts of our larger cities into new subdivisions.

Naturally, since these owners of new homes tend to be white, Protestant, middle- and upper-class Americans, the old-line Protestant churches have felt constrained to provide church facilities for them. Many of these families are too

young to have advanced far enough up the vocational ladder
to have much money left over for the church, especially after
meeting the monthly payments on a house, car, and furniture. But, they do have children who need Sunday-school
facilities. (The needs and wants of these newcomers to
suburbia lead one to suggest that possibly the VA and FHA
have encouraged the purchase of homes by persons who have
neither the financial resources nor the maturity necessary for
homeownership.) This demand for new suburban churches
has strained the financial and ministerial reserve of most
denominations to the point where only limited resources are
left for helping to develop new patterns of operations for
the old churches in rapidly changing rural and inner-city
areas.

It is only a slight exaggeration to say that the VA and
FHA have dictated how and where Protestantism should
spend its home missionary monies.

Possibly the most serious effect of this trend is that several
Protestant denominations, by placing their major evangelical
emphasis on new suburban churches, have been appealing to
a very narrow sector of American society. Only about one
third of the population can afford to live in these new homes.
In general they represent a very small portion of the total
population in terms of economic status, education level,
and social class. Whether this inbreeding will impair the
ability of the various old-line denominations to make a
universal appeal with their message about Christ and the
good news is a matter of real concern.

Here again the story is still incomplete. It is anticipated
that America will continue to build new single-family homes
at the rate of about a million per year. Also the concept of
federal credit support for homeownership almost certainly
is here to stay. Protestantism is faced with the challenge to
build many more suburban churches during the 1960's. This

will become most obvious during the late 1960's and early 1970's when the country will be confronted with a housing boom far larger than that which occurred during the 1950's.

The Impact of Public Housing

One of the most important areas in which the actions of the federal government have resulted in a major challenge to the ministry of the Christian church is in the field of public housing. On December 31, 1964, over 650,000 families were living in low-rent, subsidized public housing scattered through approximately 1,900 communities. Although 650,000 families may seem to be a very large number, for each person living in public housing there are nineteen other Americans living in privately owned housing which the Census Bureau has classified as either "dilapidated" or "deteriorating." During the past dozen years for each public-housing apartment which has been constructed there have been 49 privately owned dwellings constructed in the United States.

While public housing often is thought of in the context of big-city life, nearly 1,500 of these 1,900 communities are located *outside* urbanized areas, and only 400 are communities which had a population of over 25,000 in 1960. One half of all units in operation are concentrated in seven states (California, Georgia, Illinois, New Jersey, New York, Pennsylvania, and Texas) and in Puerto Rico.

A brief review of the history and evolution of this program will be helpful to anyone seeking to understand the challenge public housing places before the church. Public housing as we know it began in the 1930's. The motivation was primarily the desire to create employment rather than to clear slums or to provide additional housing. In fact, there was a sizable surplus of urban housing as a result of the depression exodus from the cities back to the farms. Thus it was the Public Works Administration that began, financed, and supervised the first federally subsidized public-housing units. Under the administration's program sixty developments were built in over fifty different cities in the United States.

While the first public housing projects were temporary measures to make work, a permanent program was enacted in 1937 which emphasized slum clearance and required that one substandard dwelling be eliminated for each new unit constructed. This also meant that public housing would not increase the supply of available housing and thus would not interfere with the private-housing market. The program provided for a continuing government subsidy which enabled the local housing authorities to rent the units to low-income families who otherwise could not secure safe, sanitary, and decent housing.

The next important legislative measure was the Housing Act of 1949, which is more famous for marking the beginning of urban renewal, but which also authorized a program of 810,000 units of public housing to be built over a six-year period. Later this was drastically cut back, and the entire authorization has never been fulfilled. By late 1964, however, over 650,000 units of locally owned and operated public housing in more than 1,900 communities were under the supervision of the Public Housing Administration. As a result of the authorizations contained in the Housing Act of 1964, this number will soon increase to 776,000 units and will house about 3,000,000 persons. In Cleveland one person out of every thirty now lives in public housing, and the ratio will decline to one out of twenty-four when current projects are completed. In New York the proportion is now one person out of seventeen.

Much more significant than the legislative history of public housing have been the changes in the characteristics of the people living in public housing. In the 1930's the people who lived in public housing often were comparatively well-educated and skilled persons who were temporarily "down on their luck." Some were students. Some were unemployed or were putting in a short workweek as a result of the depression. Most of the families were comparatively young, stable, and upwardly mobile. A husband and wife in their twenties or thirties with two or three children formed the typical public-housing family.

A great many of the original residents of public housing have moved on and now hold responsible positions in our society as businessmen, teachers, lawyers, and community leaders. There was no social stigma attached to anyone living in public housing, and most people, residents and nonresidents alike, regarded this as only a temporary step in a family's life. In many respects the public housing of the 1930's paralleled the temporary veterans' housing of the post-World War II period.

Today a large proportion of the residents of public housing are what the social workers refer to as problem families. They include fatherless families, families without a full-time wage earner, or families where the breadwinner's health does not permit him to work at all. They include many of the persons who are discriminated against in our society because of race, color, or language—Puerto Ricans, Negroes, Orientals, and Mexicans. They include many who lack the occupational skills required for a steady job in the city. They include substantial numbers of low-income persons who have been displaced by urban renewal and cannot find private housing at a price near what they were paying in the slums.

Since 1956 there also has been a notable increase in the number of elderly people living in public housing. Some of the recently completed projects and many of those now under construction were planned specifically for the elderly. This is partly a result of recent federal legislation which has encouraged this emphasis and partly because local housing managers want to avoid the difficulties which accompany a large concentration of unwed mothers, broken homes, and other problem families. Another reason is political expediency. It is easier to find a site for a new project if the neighbors are assured that the residents will be elderly people rather than fatherless children and unwed mothers.

Site selection has proved to be one of the biggest problems confronting public housing. In many communities some type of referendum must be held before the local housing authority can proceed. While a majority may favor the idea of public housing, no one wants the project near his home. This issue has been further complicated by the use of public housing as a means for relocating low-income Negroes who have been displaced by slum-clearance or freeway-construction projects.

The two most common answers have followed the path of least political resistance. The first and still most widely accepted solution was to build the new projects in or near existing slums, thus concentrating an additional large number of problem families in an area which already had too many such residents.

Frequently these new projects have actually been expansions of old public-housing developments, or they have been built immediately adjacent to previously constructed public-housing apartments. In either case the net result is the creation of huge institutionlike developments housing three, four, or five thousand families. Thus in one single area there will be a concentration of 8,000 to 20,000 people made up exclusively of public-housing residents.

It is hardly surprising that this prisonlike atmosphere has had demoralizing effects on the people. This certainly has been a factor in the increase in social disorganization, delinquency, and crime.

The fear of public housing and what a new project might

bring is shared by many residents who live in or near slum neighborhoods. Frequently they do not want public housing to be erected in their area either, but often they lack the political effectiveness of their wealthier neighbors. Therefore, a sense of unwantedness is communicated clearly to the residents of public-housing projects, both old and new. The residents are aware of this and reflect it.

This is the situation into which the church is called to create a community of believers. This is the forgotten frontier of Protestantism.

The challenge to Protestantism is threefold. First is the church's ministry to the people who live in this social and economic ghetto which public housing has become. Unlike many other communities, where people go to church on their own initiative, the experience of pastors suggests that in public housing the church must go to the people.

Those churches which appear to be most effective have ministers who have the opportunity and inclination to spend much time in calling, in leading Bible study groups in project apartments, in street-corner conversations, and in similar face-to-face contacts on the residents' own grounds.

Frequently this type of ministry involves services outside the conventional range. One church has a full-time dietitian on the staff to help residents learn the basic skills of homemaking. Another has a youth worker who spends most of his time diverting youthful energies from gang warfare to athletic contests. Another church offers a comprehensive after-school program which includes Christian education, recreation, and counseling. Other churches have arranged summer vacations for "project kids," during which time public-housing children spend a few weeks with a farm or suburban family and get a glimpse of a wholly new world. Nearly every pastor who serves the residents of a public-housing development agrees that pastoral counseling constitutes a large and time-consuming portion of his ministry.

Such experiences point out the urgency for the church to go out and live the gospel in the midst of a public-housing project. When this has been done the door is opened, at least part way, for the preaching of the word and the administration of the sacraments.

The second part of the challenge involves the general area of church administration and may require the church to discard some of its stereotypes. First is the concept that every local church should be self-supporting. Families living in public housing are not financially independent. By definition they require publicly subsidized housing or they could not remain in the project. Frequently they are dependent on outside assistance for food, clothing, and other necessities. It is unlikely that they will be able to support their own church. Furthermore, there is the real question of whether a check from a public welfare agency should include a sum for the church.

This issue is compounded by the fact that these people not only have little money but also have a deficit of leadership and church skills. The answer is for the church to have a multiple staff. In general, Protestantism has reserved the concept of a multiple staff either for large churches which can afford such a staff or for a few subsidized institutional churches.

If the challenge of public housing is to be met, many local churches will have to be involved, and the staff will have to get out of the building and go into the projects. This will require a heavy and continuing financial subsidy by the church at large.

Traditionally a church serving 200 to 300 families has only one full-time professional person on the staff, but experience to date indicates that a church seeking to serve that number of public-housing families should have three full-time professional staff members. The intensity of the pastoral care responsibility makes it impossible to do the job with fewer people. Ministers must do more than call only when someone is sick or when someone seeks statistics on religious preferences.

This requires a far different ratio of ministers or churches to people than now prevails in most public housing areas. In most suburban areas there is one Protestant church for every 1,000 to 1,500 residents. In rural areas and in many parts of the South there often is one Protestant church for every 200 to 500 persons. In most parts of the inner city one will encounter a church, including storefronts, for every 400 to 700 inhabitants.

How does this compare with public-housing neighborhoods? In St. Louis one densely populated census tract contains 12,500 people living in public-housing projects. Half of the people in that census tract receive some form of public assistance. In one of the projects over one half of the families do not have a father living with them. There are three Protestant churches in the area to minister to these people, plus the 8,000 nearby residents living in private housing—and one church does not have a building. A survey of religious preferences revealed that the 417 persons who stated a Protestant preference attended 132 different churches.

In Cleveland one 500-family project houses 2,000 people —and one main-line Protestant church is attempting to provide a pastoral ministry to them and to 13,000 other nearby residents. In another project only one Protestant church is attempting to carry on a full-scale ministry to the 3,000 residents, and that chuch is housed in a storefront.

Recently a sample survey of religious activity in that neighborhood revealed that 283 persons identified themselves as Protestant, but only 187 of these had any kind of relationship with a local church—and they named 101 churches! The most popular church had eighteen adherents, the second most popular had twelve, and the third most popular drew only six residents. More than 60 per cent of the churches were three or four miles away.

Such results are in sharp contrast to the findings of similar surveys in suburbia, where a majority of the churchgoers identify with one of the churches located within their community.

It also will be necessary to reshape some of our tools and techniques of Christian education. Some of the Sunday-school material that is built around Dick and Jane in their happy home will have to be replaced by something that is more relevant to the lives of project children.

The third aspect of the challenge of public housing to the church concerns the social implications of the gospel. There are many profound moral questions involved in public housing. What is the best location for new sites, in the middle of existing slums or in open land on the periphery of the city? How large should a project be? Are the social problems magnified by concentrating 500 or 1,000 problem families in a fifteen to fifty-acre area? Does the current emphasis on public housing for the aged discriminate against the hundreds of thousands of younger families who are unable to find safe, sanitary, and decent housing at a price they can afford? Is it good for elderly couples and individuals to be segregated from other age groups in our society? Does public housing help relieve and eliminate conditions of social disorganization, or does it encourage an irresponsible attitude? Should future additions to the supply of public housing be confined to very small, widely scattered units? (This has been tried in Philadelphia and a few other cities with promising results.) Has the design of projects contributed to the institutional character of public housing?

These and similar questions demand answers. The society which has created public housing must provide the answers.

The Impact of the Expressways

The challenge presented by public housing demands a response from many churches, perhaps as many as 10,000 to 25,000 individual congregations are or should be involved in this specialized ministry. Far more impressive from a statistical point of view is the emerging network of expressways. The total capital investment in the expressway program is more than five times the capital investment in public housing. While less than 5 per cent of all churches in the United States will be involved in a ministry to residents of public housing, at least three or four times that figure will be affected by the expressway program—a program which was made possible only through the resources and influence of the federal government.

Adoption of the Federal Aid Highway Act in the United States in 1956 launched a 50,000,000,000-dollar program intended to connect nearly all the major cities of America. Known as the Interstate Highway System, this is said to be the most extensive and expensive public-works program in history. Approximately one half of this system is now in use. The target date for completion is 1972. While most of the mileage is to be built in rural areas, one half of the money will be spent in the urban centers which are connected by the system.

This program is complicating life for hundreds of Protestant churches in scores of metropolitan areas and in hundreds of smaller communities.

Enough time has passed so that it is now possible to begin to evaluate the impact of expressways on the church. Are these new highways assets or liabilities? Do they hinder or do they assist the church in fulfilling its mission? How are they affecting the plans churchmen make for the future of Protestantism in America?

Perhaps the most important single characteristic of the expressways is that they were not intended to be barriers dividing neighborhoods, but were planned to serve as channels for moving people and goods more quickly from one place to another. This is sometimes overlooked as people contemplate the width of the right-of-way, the height of the entrance ramps, or the depth of the cut for a depressed roadway. Seen from this latter perspective the expressway may appear to be an overwhelming divisive force rather than a new dimension in church planning.

If viewed in more dynamic terms, however, the expressway can be seen as an integrating force which facilitates the maintenance of membership loyalties. The exodus to suburbia meant that millions of Protestants moved out of the old neighborhoods to new homes on the outskirts of the city. For a few months they may have faithfully returned every Sunday to their old church home, but frequently this involved a thirty- or forty-minute drive through city traffic. All too often the nerve-wracking rush to get the family ready for church on Sunday morning plus the struggle with traffic offset the attachment to the church, and the new suburbanite either transferred to a nearby church or just dropped out of the churchgoing habit.

The coming of the expressways has altered this problem. If the city has a good network of limited access, high-speed highways, a church member can move to almost any neighborhood in the community and still be within reasonable driving distance of his old church.

Expressways have added a new dimension to the traditional parish boundaries. One result is that they may be a vital factor in prolonging the life of older congregations.

There are a number of serious implications to this emerging trend, however.

First, this raises the question of the place of the geographical parish. Is it a healthy trend which sees so many churches moving away from their historic role as "neighborhood churches"? Can Protestantism be an effective evangelical force if each local church becomes a "gathered congregation," bringing people together from all over the entire metropolitan area?

Who will do the hard work of neighborhood evangelism? Can a pastor find enough hours in the week to visit the members of a far-flung congregation and still call door-to-door in the neighborhood of the church? If not which will get priority?

A second problem is the advisability of encouraging members to continue their membership after they have moved away. While there is no question that it is very comforting to come back every Sunday to see familiar faces in familiar surroundings, there is a real question as to the effect this has on the people who are moving into the neighborhood around the church.

Will the old-timers really welcome the newcomers? Or will the newcomers feel they are intruders in a private club? Will the old members willingly relinquish positions of leadership to new members? Or do they continue to return every week primarily because they hold positions of authority?

Closely related is the impact of this trend on the policies and practices of the local church. For example, if a church becomes increasingly dependent on nonresident members, this means that adequate parking must be available or the advantages of expressway travel will be negated.

Will the congregation buy the house next door to the church, raze it, and pave the lot for parking? Or will they remodel the house and use it for church-school and neighborhood youth activities? If a second minister is to be called will the congregation seek someone who is skilled in neighborhood evangelism? Or will they prefer someone who will be more comfortable calling on the older, scattered members? Questions such as these must be faced by congregations which find expressways to be a means for retaining the loyalty of members who are moving out of the church's neighborhood.

There is another area in which expressways are adding a new dimension to Protestant church planning, however. This concerns the choice of church sites. In the old days the primary consideration in selecting a church site, whether for a new congregation or for one which was relocating, has been concerned with the neighborhood. How many people live within walking distance of the site? What was the anticipated population growth for the area? How many churches were already in the community? These are the kinds of questions which traditionally have been asked by a site selection committee.

The emergence of the expressways is altering this thinking. In nearly every large city there are two, three, or a half dozen very large congregations which draw members from all parts of the metropolis. Most churches, however, were content to be neighborhood institutions serving a relatively small number of people.

The expressways have added a new dimension to this picture. While land near the expressway usually is not cheap, the price is often low enough that a congregation can afford to buy three to ten acres, thus providing room for a building and a parking lot. Such a site is as good as if not better than a downtown location for a group seeking to include the entire metropolitan area within the church's parish.

This is the newest development in the church location picture. Thus far this practice has been confined largely to denominations which have only one congregation in the metropolitan area. Increasingly, however, one can find examples of denominational churches which are seeking the advantages of an expressway location regardless of the effect this may have on other churches of their own fellowship.

This trend toward utilizing the advantages of an expressway system in selecting a church site runs directly counter to the thinking of most denominational officials who have long accepted the validity of the geographical parish and have urged an appropriate geographical spacing of churches on the premise that each will serve a limited area.

If each congregation choosing an expressway location expects to serve a drive-in congregation made up of residents from all parts of the metropolis—and this is the most logical reason for selecting a site adjacent to a noisy expressway—many of the traditional premises used in denominational and interdenominational church planning must be discarded. Thus far few churchmen have recognized this challenge to traditional planning principles.

These illustrations of the impact of policies and actions by the federal government offer convincing evidence of the role of one external force which exerts great influence on church planning at both the congregational and the denominational levels of church administration.

The record of the past is clear. What then does the future hold? In general terms the answer is clear. As the role of the federal government becomes ever more important in the economic and social aspects of American life, so will the church be increasingly affected—especially in its institutional life. The effect of this influence can be seen more easily by looking backward than by looking forward. During the nineteenth century the Homestead Act, the land grants to railroads, the purchase of the Louisiana Territory, and the decisions to abolish slavery and to use force to prevent the secession of states from the union were some of the governmental decisions which had a major effect on the life and work of Protestant churches. Recognition of the impact of governmental decisions on the church's past should encourage churchmen to study carefully current and proposed federal programs in order to determine their effect on church planning.

During the past years the actions of the federal government, including those of the Supreme Court, have been the crucial element in the whole field of race relations. The ramifications in the area of church planning are clear and cannot be ignored. Henceforth Protestants *must* plan to minister to all persons regardless of differences in skin color. The biblical imperative has been reinforced by the policies and actions of the federal government.

During the coming years the actions of the federal government will affect the church in many ways. Almost certainly financial aid for hospitals, homes for the aged, higher education, and public housing will increase. The church should be prepared to define its relationship to these enlarged programs. They already have had substantial impact on the plans of many church-related colleges and hospitals and other religious institutions. This impact will be even greater in the years to come.

Finally it should be noted that the policies of the federal government have influenced the work of the church by determining to which section of the country people will be moving. The Homestead Act had this effect in the nineteenth century, but its twentieth-century counterpart is more complex.

The decision as to whether a multibillion dollar defense contract will be awarded to a firm in Texas, Georgia, Kansas, or California is an obvious example. Less obvious in its implications was the adoption of the Social Security Act, which a quarter of a century later makes it financially feasible for literally thousands of retired persons to leave behind the cold winters of New York, Ohio, and Wisconsin and migrate to Florida, Arizona, and California. The federally financed space age not only has resulted in the creation of whole new cities in Texas, Alabama, and Florida, but it also causes many families to move to Massachusetts, New York, and California.

This account of the different ways in which the actions of the national government affect the church makes one wonder if the alleged "wall of separation" is more a figure of speech than a fact of American life. Congress may not make any laws respecting the establishment of a religion, but it certainly has enacted a great many affecting the plans and actions of Protestantism!

While the actions of state and local governments have not had the widespread impact on church planning that the decisions emanating from Washington have, they are factors which must be reckoned with in planning for the future of the church.

Perhaps the most important example is the post World War II trend in school consolidations. These changes have drastically altered community boundaries, and one result is that many circuits which include two, three, or four churches should be realigned in accordance with changing social relationships. In other cases the consolidations of rural schools point the way to the consolidation of small rural churches.

In addition, there are a variety of other issues confronting the church planners in which the policies and decisions of state or local officials will be an important factor in developing a planning program. Will the board of education allow this new congregation to rent the auditorium of a public school until they are strong enough to build their church? If parsonages are not exempt from the general property tax is it advisable to pay a housing allowance rather than to buy a parsonage? Will the board of zoning appeals permit the church to develop a parking lot on the vacant property across the street? Does the policy on special assessments for water, sewer, street improvements, and sidewalks make it inadvisable for the small congregation to purchase a corner lot? If the new off-street parking ordinance requires one parking space for each three seats in the largest room can the inner-city church afford to enlarge and remodel its building, or must it relocate? Does the building code make it impossible to benefit from the economies that go with prefabricated construction? How far in advance of the actual transfer of property must a denomination commit itself if it seeks to purchase a church site in an urban renewal area? These are but a few of the questions asked of public officials.

Governmental actions are not the only external forces which influence church planning. Anyone attempting to develop a realistic program for the future of the church must also take into consideration a wide variety of social and economic factors. One of the most important of these is the implications of recent population changes.

Implications of Population Trends [1]

Whenever a group of active churchmen gather and begin to talk about the population explosion the listener can expect to hear a variety of comments. A pastor may explain that each year in the United States one person in five moves and

---

[1] Most of the census data used in this chapter can be found in either *Statistical Abstract of the United States, 1962* (Washington: U. S. Department of Commerce, Bureau of the Census, 1962) or *Historical Statistics of the United States, Colonial Times to 1957* (Washington: U. S. Department of Commerce, Bureau of the Census, 1960). These two volumes are essential tools for the demographer or the church planner. For an excellent analysis of the changes in the birth cycle see Richard A. Easterlin, *The American Baby Boom in Historical Perspective* (New York: National Bureau of Economic Research, 1962).

thus the average church can expect a 100 per cent turnover in membership every five years. Someone may comment on the fact that in 1961 for the first time in history the population of the United States increased at a faster pace than did membership in Protestant churches, and he may use this to support his contention that Christianity is on the decline in America. Someone else may explain that membership in the Catholic Church is increasing more rapidly than in Protestant churches because the Catholic birthrate is higher than for any Protestant body. If the conversation shifts to the neglected areas of the inner city someone may remark about the need for a mission to minister to "alcoholics on Skid Row."

Comments such as these have been heard by every active churchman who is interested in the changes which are occurring in America's population. In addition to their familiarity, all the observations mentioned above share one other common characteristic. *Each one is either a false statement or is very misleading.*

Collectively they reflect the influence which population trends should have on church planning, but they also emphasize the need for anyone concerned with church planning to be extremely wary of demographic statistics.

Before turning to an examination of the population explosion an explanation should be offered concerning the statements in the opening paragraph of this chapter.

While it is true that approximately 20 per cent of the people move each year, *this does not mean that the American people move on the average of once every five years.* In fact, it is essentially the same small group of people who do most of the moving. Some people move every year or two; others stay in the same house for decades. Approximately one half of the American people stay in the same house for at least five years, and nearly four fifths of these live in the same house for ten or more years.

Thus a Protestant congregation which is representative of the total population in this respect can expect about one fifth of their members to change addresses every year, but they also can expect one half of their members to stay put for at least five years.

Furthermore, merely because a person moves to a different house does not mean he will join a different church. Two thirds of all moves find the person moving to a different house but staying within the same county. In an average year only 6 per cent of the people move out of the county in which they have been living. For most churches this means that many of the moves of members will take them from one house to another, but they will stay within the geographical parish of the same local church.

Finally it should be noted that the categories of the population from which main-line Protestant churches draw many of their members move less frequently than the average for the entire population. The mobility rate of farmers is one half that of the total population. White-collar employees move less often than do blue-collar employees. Whites do not move as often as Negroes. Persons who have passed their thirty-fifth birthdays move less often than do younger persons. Suburbanites move less often than do the residents of the central city.

A pastor can expect many of his members to change their addresses during the year, but if a different one fifth of his congregation moves every year he has a most unusual group of Christians in his church.

It is also true that in 1961 the American population grew at a more rapid pace than did Protestant church membership. As Philip J. Allen has pointed out, however, *the important relationship is between changes in church member-*

ship and changes in that segment of the population old enough to be church members.[2] If this becomes the basis for calculating comparative statistics it is clear that church membership growth has almost exactly paralleled population growth in the age-twelve-and-over category. Furthermore, if one could adjust the statistics to allow for the financial pressures which have induced many local churches to clean their membership rolls, the results probably would indicate that evangelism efforts are more than keeping abreast of population changes.

The comment on the high Catholic birthrate was valid a generation ago. According to a special census made in 1957, however, the church body with the highest birthrate was not the Catholics; it was the Baptists. The results of this census indicated quite clearly that the rural-urban characteristic is probably the most important single factor in determining the birthrate of a religious body. Therefore, it is not surprising that Baptists, being the most rural of all religious groups in America, should have the highest birthrate.

The idea that Skid Row is inhabited only by winos, alcoholics, and drunkards is another demographic illusion. Perhaps the most careful statistical study of the habits and characteristics of the residents of Skid Row ever undertaken was recently completed in Chicago. This study found that only 12.6 per cent of the men on Skid Row could be classified as alcoholics and another 19.9 per cent as "heavy drinkers," while 43.1 per cent were either teetotalers or light drinkers. It was also significant that the heaviest drinkers were the best educated while those with limited formal education tended to be either teetotalers or light drinkers. The study suggested that men live on Skid Row, not because they are alcoholics, but rather because there they can find low

[2] "Let's Be Precise!" ("Letters to the Editor") *The Christian Century* (March 6, 1963), p. 304.

living costs, a market for unskilled labor, anonymity, toler-
ance, companionship, and welfare services.[3] Anyone planning
to bring the ministry of Jesus Christ to men on Skid Row
should be concerned primarily with the problems of poverty
and personal disorganization rather than with alcoholism.

These illustrations show how easy it is to misconstrue
population statistics and how careful use of available data
will help one to avoid misleading stereotypes. Responsible
and effective planning for the future requires that demographic figures be used with discrimination and care. Frequently statistics and references to population changes can
be properly understood and accurately interpreted only if
considered from a historical perspective. The best illustration of this is the widely publicized "population explosion."

The nationwide attention given the increase in population
has influenced church planning—but this does not mean that
churches have comprehended the basic nature of the so-called
population explosion.

Perhaps the most helpful way to describe and analyze increase in population is by reviewing four periods of population growth in America. The first ran from 1909 to 1927.
During that period the increase in the nation's residents was
almost exactly offset by a decline in the birthrate, and as
a result the number of children born each year leveled off at
a figure which ranged from 2,700,000 to 3,000,000. This
trend prevailed long enough for people to become accus-
tomed to this rate of growth. Therefore, it was something of
a shock when this trend was replaced in the new period which
lasted from 1928 to 1939 during which the number of babies
born each year dropped to the 2,300,000 to 2,500,000 level.
This of course was a result of a continued decline in the
birthrate which more than offset the increase in the number

[3] *The Homeless Man on Skid Row* (Chicago: The Tenants Relocation
Bureau of the City of Chicago, September, 1961), pp. 7, 18, 19.

of persons of childbearing age. Many demographers construed this to be a permanent trend and predicted a leveling off in the population growth curve of America.

Many of them made these predictions in the face of a third trend which began in 1940 and saw the annual number of births hover around the 3,500,000 level. The experts regarded this as a temporary baby boom directly related to World War II, and they predicted that it was only a temporary departure from a long-term trend which would see the births figure drop back to about 3,000,000 per year.

As everyone now knows the demographers failed to outguess the stork. Instead of going down the number of births leveled off until 1951—and then it went up! A new plateau was being established. In 1954 the 4,000,000 mark was reached, and during the following decade the number of babies born each year ranged from 4,000,000 to 4,300,000—a figure 50 per cent above the average for the previous half century. By 1970 this plateau will have been raised to 5,000,000, and it may reach the 6,000,000 level before 1980.

This appraisal of recent vital statistics clearly reveals that the population explosion was not a temporary phenomenon of the decade following Pearl Harbor. Rather the so-called explosion was a force which has had a permanent influence, for it marked the end of one era of stability and the beginning of a new era of rapid growth.

This is an extremely important consideration for anyone involved in planning for the future of Protestantism in America, for such planning should use the dynamic years of 1945-60 as a reference point rather than the static years of 1930-45. This is easier to say than to practice; for many of the leaders and decision makers in Protestant churches the 1930-40 era was the time of their formative years, and they will be inclined to view that period as "normal" and the 1950's as "abnormal." An examination of the population explosion from a historical perspective reveals that just the opposite is true, but this may not change the frame of reference of some of the older leaders and powers.

In addition to looking at population trends from a historical perspective it is also helpful to interpret them from the point of view of the church. Frequently such an interpretation will reveal implications that were not apparent at first.

An example of this is the rather well-publicized fact that over one half (1,580 of 3,072) of all counties in the United States experienced a net population loss during the 1950 to 1960 decade. This was usually interpreted as a population trend of importance primarily for denominational town and country commissions. If one looks more carefully at these statistics, however, it is possible to derive additional insights which have major significance in church planning.

First of all, it should be noted that two thirds of the counties losing population were located in fifteen states— Texas, 145; Georgia, 97; Kentucky, 87; Missouri, 86; Nebraska, 74; Kansas, 71; Oklahoma, 65; Iowa, 62; Mississippi, 61; Tennessee, 59; Virginia, 45; Alabama, 45; West Virginia, 44; North Dakota, 42; and South Dakota, 42. These states share several common characteristics. All are predominantly Protestant; most had a large Negro population in 1950; and most were and still are basically rural states. With a couple of exceptions the largest denominations in these states have been the Baptists, Methodists, and Christians, while denominations such as the Congregational Christian, Lutheran, Episcopal, Evangelical United Brethren, United Presbyterian, U. S. A., and Evangelical and Reformed are comparatively weak. Finally a detailed examination of the figures reveals that most of the counties losing population were rural counties.

What does this say to the church planner? It says that this

decline is a subject of greatest interest to the town and country commissions of three church bodies (Baptist, Methodist, and Christian) and is of comparatively minor importance to the town and country leaders of other denominations which have few churches in these declining counties. The figures also indicate that *all* denominations should be interested in another dimension of this trend. Where did the people go who left these Midwest and Southern rural counties? For the most part they went to the cities of the North, the Northwest, and the Pacific Coast. In these areas all the denominations mentioned earlier are comparatively strong. A large percentage of these rural migrants, both Negro and white, moved into the central city of these metropolitan areas and replaced the older residents who moved to suburbia. Thus a population trend, which at first glance appeared to be of major importance only to town and country commissions, turns out to be of greater significance for the urban-life departments and for the agencies concerned with interracial issues.

Many other helpful insights emerge from a study of demographic material if examined from the perspective of the possible impact on the Protestant churches.

The growth of suburbia and the growing activity of church extension agencies in Protestantism have caused many Protestant leaders to focus their attention on this aspect of the population explosion and its impact on the church. Inasmuch as most Protestant churches still have a strong family orientation, the number of families or households becomes the most useful yardstick in measuring church extension needs. In order to obtain comparable historical data the accompanying table lists both families and households (basically this is a housing unit figure which includes persons living alone in apartments or a group of unrelated persons living together, while family involves a blood or marriage relationship.)

NUMBER OF HOUSEHOLDS AND FAMILIES[4]
(In thousands)

Year	Households	Families
1900	15,992	n.a.
1920	24,467	n.a.
1930	29,997	n.a.
1940	35,153	n.a.
1945	37,503	n.a.
1950	43,554	39,303
1955	47,788	41,934
1960	52,610	45,062
1965	56,076	48,133
1970	61,094	52,149
1975	69,318	56,963
1980	76,006	62,212

The figures in this table explain why church extension became a major concern of Protestantism in the 1945-60 period. New households were being created at an average rate of over 1,000,000 per year. The figures also explain why church extension efforts, except for some catching up with the backlog of need, were somewhat in a lull during the 1960-65 period. This was only a temporary breathing spell, however, for the late 1960's and all the 1970's will require an unprecedented level of activity if the needs of the people as represented by additional households or families are to be served. If the same ratio of churches to families is to be maintained Protestants should plan that for every three new churches organized in the 1960-65 years, four must be developed in the 1965-70 period and five during the 1970-75

---

[4] Projections for 1965-80 are the Series B estimates made by the Bureau of the Census.

era. If one uses a church-household ratio the figures change to 3.5, 5, and 8 respectively, an even greater challenge! In addition, the impact of this growth will be magnified by the continuing clustering of people in the large urban centers which grow at a faster pace than the national average.

The changes in the age composition of the population also have important implications for Protestant churches.

A frequent complaint of pastors is, "We are short of leaders, especially younger ones." During the present decade this condition will become more acute as the number of persons age sixty and over increases from 24,000,000 in 1963 to 28,500,000 in 1970—thus increasing the supply of older leaders. However, the number of persons in the 35-44-year-old bracket—the age group which produces leaders with both maturity and vision—will decline from 24,400,000 in 1963 to 23,100,000 in 1970, and they will be distributed among a larger number of churches. This reflects the decline in total births mentioned earlier which began in 1928 and ran through 1939. This same manpower shortage will also confront the pulpit committee looking for "a dynamic and experienced pastor in his late thirties or early forties." The demand for this type of leadership, both lay and ministerial, will be greater because of the additional new congregations being organized, but the supply will be smaller.

On the other hand, a number of religious institutions will be under new pressures because of unprecedented demands. One of these is church-related homes for the elderly, which, because of available governmental assistance in financing, are now being planned and constructed at a comparatively rapid pace.

Church-school facilities will again be in short supply as the number of five- to fourteen-year-olds increases from the 35,700,000 total of 1960 to 39,200,000 in 1965 and 41,000,000 in 1970.

Protestant seminaries, which have experienced a decline in enrollment during the past few years, should plan for large entering classes in the late 1960's as the number of twenty-two-year-old men (the usual age for beginning seminarians) jumps from 1,200,000 in 1963 to 1,400,000 in 1967 and to 1,800,000 in 1969. If the same proportion of young men enter seminary in both years the entering class of 1969 should be 50 per cent larger than the entering class in 1963. The graduating class of 1980 should be 70 per cent larger than the graduating class of 1965. During this same fifteen-year period, however, the number of persons old enough to be members (twelve and over) of Protestant churches will increase by only 23 per cent. At first glance it would appear that the current shortage of ministers could turn into a sur-plus within a relatively few years. This is unlikely, however, because of several counterforces. The improved pension systems will encourage earlier retirements; an increasing number of ministers will be called for staff positions in the denominational and interdenominational bureaucracy of the church; the number of full-time supply pastors will be reduced; and more churches will turn to a multiple staff system utilizing the services of two, three, or four ministers. These four factors alone probably will cause the demand to equal or exceed the supply.

Church-related colleges and universities already are beginning to feel the pressures of increased enrollments, but the biggest strain will come in 1965, when the number of eighteen-year-olds jumps from the 2,700,000, level of 1963 to 3,700,000 in 1965—a 37 per cent increase in two years!

In addition, a careful analysis of statistics and trends will reveal several other areas in which population changes may have a major influence on the plans of Protestants. In some of these the effect on the church is more obvious than it is in others. For example, the challenge posed by the migration of thousands of Negroes from the rural South to the urban North cannot be missed. The church has been slow to react, however, to the greater emphasis on postgraduate training which is requiring more young men and women to remain in school until their middle or late twenties. This is a rapidly growing segment of the nation's population. The enrollment of colleges, universities, and professional schools is expected to rise from 4,000,000 in 1960 to 7,800,000 in 1970 and to 11,500,000 in 1980. Are the old concepts of a campus ministry adequate for these students, many of whom are married and have children? Should the church plan to provide a more mature church experience for these career students? Perhaps this should be the same type of church relationship that is available to their friends of the same age who are employed in commerce, industry, or government.

The needs of the rapidly growing ranks of senior citizens have received considerable attention from those who are charged with the responsibility of planning the program offerings of Protestantism, but little attention has been paid to the religious needs of the growing ranks of the unemployed. What kind of doctrine of work will the church preach to the chronically unemployed, to the high-school dropout who cannot find a steady job, to the forty-eight-year-old flight engineer or the fifty-three-year-old machinist who have seen their jobs eliminated through technological advances?

All across America plans are being made to minister to the family moving into a new suburban home. These plans are all predicated on the assumption that this family will live in that home seven days a week and fifty weeks a year. Very few church leaders have recognized that the shortened work-week, longer vacations, higher incomes, and earlier retirements mean that this family may be spending a good many Sundays out of the year at their vacation home in the mountains or at the lake. Who is planning to minister to the two-house family?

In the Great Commission the disciples of Christ are charged with the responsibility of going out into the world and preaching the gospel to all creation. Implementation of that commission in urban America means that this mission must be planned carefully if it is to succeed in reaching *all* God's children. This planning requires that population statistics and trends must be carefully studied and interpreted from the perspective of both history and the mission of the church.

This discussion of the influence of governmental actions and population changes is not intended to be definitive but only to illustrate the impact of external forces on the plans and programs of Protestantism. The churchman must reckon with other forces besides these, however, for he is not helping to plan for the future of just another institution; he is trying to help build the kingdom of God. In this task he must bring together an awareness of the influence of a variety of forces. He must be able to combine planning skills with theological insights, and this can be accomplished only through a marriage of the two.

3

The Courtship of Theology
and Planning
+++

MOST OF THE OBSERVATIONS ON CHURCH PLANNING MADE IN the earlier two chapters are based on the knowledge and insights gained by planners employed in secular fields. This is justifiable, for churchmen and religious organizations have contributed little to our understanding of the dynamics of planning. Many of the techniques and understandings developed by city planners are basic to any church-planning operation. These would include, among others, methods of population analysis, land-use studies, physical site planning and the role of planning in the total administrative process. Furthermore, members of the planning profession are continually proposing new ideas which will improve the quality and increase the relevance of planning. On the other hand, the committed Christian has resources on which he can draw that can be utilized to develop a more profound understanding of the planning process, the role of the planner, and the goals of church planning.

Perhaps the most exciting development in city planning today is the emergence of Constantinos Apostolos Doxiadis and his doctrine of *Ekistics* (the science of human settlements). Traditionally city planning has been based on the design of the physical environment and has been concerned primarily with things rather than with people. This has made planning vulnerable to both mistakes and criticism. *Ekistics* broadens the approach to planning by bringing in sociologists, economists, geographers, political scientists, and mathematicians. While Doxiadis' theories have not won anything approaching universal acceptance, it is inevitable that his and similar proposals will broaden the conceptual framework of city planning and radically change the approach of some planners.

It is also significant that the most widely read and hotly discussed book ever published on the subject of city planning in America has as its basic theme the failure of city planners to comprehend the needs of people as individuals and as members of social groups. This book, *The Death and Life of Great American Cities*[1] by Jane Jacobs, has received a strongly negative reaction from most planners but has been widely acclaimed by lay observers and a few planners.[2] In it the author contends that the planner should be an ecologist and that city planning should be oriented to the relationship

---

[1] New York: Random House, Inc., 1961. See also Edward J. Logue and Edward T. Chase, "American Cities: Dead or Alive?—Two Views," *Architectural Forum* (March, 1962), pp. 89-91.

[2] See Dennis O'Harrow, "Jacobin Revival," in the American Society of Planning Officials *Newsletter* (February, 1962); Roger Starr, "Adventure in Mooritania," in the *Newsletter* of the Citizen's Housing and Planning Council of New York (January, 1962); and John A. Kouwenhoven's review in the *New York Herald-Tribune* book review section (November 3, 1961), p. 8.

between people and their environment which includes other people as well as buildings, streets, et cetera.

This is not a completely new idea by any means, but never before has it been expressed in such forceful language. Quite naturally it has aroused a highly defensive reaction among design-oriented planners. Traditionally city planners have been trained in physical design—architecture, engineering, and landscape architecture—and by virtue of their training have helped to perpetuate this emphasis on a narrow definition of the city and of city planning. The contributions of Doxiadis and Jacobs, however, are hopeful signs that the old saying, "Planning is for people," will cease to be a meaningless cliché and become an influential guide for city planners. Perhaps even more exciting, and certainly more rapid, are the changes which are occurring in the field of church planning. This discipline is even younger than city planning, but in recent years it has been undergoing changes of a greater magnitude which are having a heavier impact than have the influences affecting city planners.

As city planning had its early beginnings in the work of architects and landscape architects, church planning traces its origins back to the contributions of sociologists. The first handbook or guide in local church planning was published as recently as 1915.[3] For many years descriptive surveys constituted all that might be called "church planning." As time went by the quality of the surveys improved tremendously. Churchmen such as H. Paul Douglass, Edmund deS. Brunner, Ross W. Sanderson, and Murray H. Leiffer made important contributions both in methodology and in the training of men to work in the field of religious research and survey.

Concurrently with the emergence of church surveys came the rise of "comity." This was a proposal which provided for

[3] Charles E. Carroll, *The Community Survey in Relation to Church Efficiency* (New York: The Abingdon Press).

interdenominational cooperation and agreement before a denomination would initiate a new work in any area. Gradually it became apparent that if comity approval was to be won, the denomination seeking approval would be well advised to prepare a brief supporting its application. Many of these briefs were of remarkably poor quality, but the comity concept did encourage a greater emphasis on the preparation and use of religious surveys. (See Chapter 4 for a more detailed history and analysis of comity.)

The next step in the evolution of church planning was the recognition that if this new discipline was to merit use of the word "planning" it must be related more closely to the decision-making center on a continuing basis. Thus in the 1950's research and planning agencies were created which had the joint responsibility of survey and of planning. Some of these were a part of the denominational structure; some were in state or local councils of churches. The emergence of such agencies made it possible for the researcher to work on a continuing basis rather than as a one-shot consultant with the denominational decision makers. In more recent years a few of these agencies placed their primary emphasis on the dynamics of the planning process and became, in fact, church *planning* offices. Research and survey constituted an important part of the total work program of the staff, but there was a continuing relationship between the church *planner* and the decision makers, at both the denominational and local-church levels.

During the entire evolutionary process described above the overwhelming emphasis was on the church as an institution in society. It was described in primarily sociological terms (what other objective yardsticks could be used?), and even today most of the work of the church planner is directed toward the church in its institutional form. The location and timing of new suburban churches; the merger, relocation, or dissolution of inner-city churches; the possibility of building new churches in urban renewal areas; and the impact of secular forces (new highways, public housing, unemployment, slum clearance, and the rural-to-urban population movement) —these are the subjects which engage the attention of the church planner today.

Thus far almost all the evolutionary changes in church planning have emphasized the word "planning," and the efforts of most churchmen in this field have been toward improving both the mechanics and the dynamics of planning. This has been necessary, and much has been accomplished, although there remains a great deal of room for improvement in both techniques and administrative interrelationships and understandings.

A new school of thought has appeared, however, and is beginning to have an impact on both secular and church planners. Most of the contributors to this new influence are men who have their formal academic training in philosophy, social ethics, and systematic theology. These "outside" observers have contributed a variety of refreshing insights which have been directed, not toward the mechanics of planning, but toward a clearer philosophical understanding of the purpose of planning. While this is an oversimplification, it may be helpful in way of explanation to say that the emphasis in church planning is now on the word "church" as a theological concept rather than on the word "planning." A parallel in secular planning is the trend which sees the job title of many planners being changed from *city* planner to *community* planner.

It must be emphasized that this movement is only in the beginning stages of what may or may not become an important long-term trend. The association of philosophers and theologians is at best only a courtship; marriage plans are not even being discussed. Furthermore, a great many planners are still completely physical design oriented and cannot comprehend how anyone from some esoteric discipline such as theology could make a positive contribution to planning. One result is that many of the contributions of the theologian are unsolicited and, therefore, lack a ready and responsive audience.

It is far too early to say what the results of the courtship may be, but thus far significant contributions have been made in at least three areas.[4]

The first of these is a greater concern with the church as a theological, rather than a sociological institution. Much of the church planning that has occurred has been organization planning. For example, the basis for developing a "master plan" for church extension in suburbia closely resembled, both in form and in presuppositions, the master plan prepared by a city for location of new fire stations or the master plan prepared by a local board of education for the location of new public-school buildings. More recently, however, the idea that the church is a religious institution has begun to penetrate these old concepts. While there is still a widespread nationalistic sentiment behind denominational church extension work, there is also a growing recognition of church extension as one means of expressing the mission of the church. Thus instead of hearing denominational officials say, "We'll organize new Methodist (or Episcopal, or Presbyterian, et cetera) churches in suburbia wherever there is a concentration of people of our denomination. We have an obligation to serve our people," one hears the denominational executive say to the church planner, "Help us dis-

[4] I am greatly indebted to Henry Kolbe of Garrett Theological Seminary, Frederick S. Carney of the Perkins School of Theology, and Stan Hallett, Director of the Department of Church Planning of the Church Federation of Greater Chicago for their provocative and constructive comments which have stimulated much of the thinking that has gone into the preparation of this chapter.

cover the areas where there is a concentration of unchurched people. We're prepared to try to serve them." Gradually the emphasis is shifting away from an eagerness to discover new church sites in areas of "high potential" to a discussion of neighborhoods of "great need." Instead of enlarging the organization, the emphasis is now often on extending the ministry. This appears to be a direct result of the recent widespread interest in the theology of the church.[5] Perhaps the most tangible evidences of this transition are (1) the increased denominational interest in the inner city, (2) the comparatively large number of new suburban churches in which 50 to 75 per cent of the members previously never had an effective church relationship.

It is impossible to record how the contemporary theological emphasis on the church has affected each of the decision makers who have responsibilities for the institutional church. From the perspective of a church planner, however, it is obvious that the collective impact has been sufficiently large to influence the basis for making ecclesiastical decisions at the denominational level.

An example of this is the growing recognition that the people who are planning for the future of the church are not involved in a strictly "businesslike" venture to which good business administrative principles can be readily applied in the same way they are applied to the administration of most institutions in society.

While the life and the work of the church has become institutionalized in many ways, the decision maker in Protestantism must remember that the church has many noninstitutional characteristics. The primary concern of the church is not to perpetuate its own life, but rather to mediate

---

[5] Perhaps the most influential recent book in this area is Gibson Winter's *The Suburban Captivity of the Churches* (New York: Doubleday & Company, Inc., 1961).

the saving grace of God as revealed in Jesus Christ. Church planning must be mission-centered rather than institution-oriented if it is to be a positive and creative response to the call of Christ. Thus the emphasis must be on planning, not for institutional growth, but rather for increasing the opportunities for an ever larger number of persons to have a firsthand religious experience. The guiding principles which are used throughout the planning process must be derived, not from concepts such as profits, economy, competition, and laissez-faire, but rather from concepts represented by words and phrases such as love, suffering servanthood, redemption, and sin.

Perhaps the clearest way to make this initial point is to say that the theologian is forever reminding the churchman that his primary concern must be, not with the church, but with the kingdom of God.

The second point at which the theologians have made an important contribution centers on the doctrine of man and the planning function. Most of the philosophical conflicts which revolve around the planning function are a result of differing doctrines on the nature of man. This is as true of secular planners as it is of church planners. This point can be illustrated by arbitrarily dividing all planners into two groups and relating each to a theological position. On the one hand, there is the group which might be labeled the Thomas Aquinas school. These persons would agree that the universe is an orderly creation governed by consistent laws in which the obligations of men can be defined with clarity through the use of reason. Many planners in this group might disagree over the effect of the fall of man on his ability to reason out his own best interest, but with this exception, they could readily accept the teachings of Thomas Aquinas. They would agree, since most planners work for a governmental body, that the state has a distinct, unique, and necessary function in man's life, and they would perhaps concur that the state has a redemptive function.

For the members of this school of thought the concept of the master plan is a wholly compatible idea, for it fits into their perception of the universe as an orderly creation governed by unchanging laws. Through reason the planner (man) can discover these laws and the appropriate goals and use them in preparing an ideal plan of action.

On the other hand, there is the group which might be described as the disciples of Reinhold Niebuhr. For this group the doctrinal emphasis is not on man's reason but on his freedom and his power of creativity. Man's ability to be conscious of himself, of the universe, and of his relationship to the universe, and his ability to realize that he is aware of this relationship causes him to seek to use his freedom and creative power to meditate and to engage in dialogue with himself concerning his relationship to the universe and to the future. Out of this dialogue with himself may come the desire to develop a master plan which would provide reassuring direction to him. Members of the Niebuhr school realize, however, that such efforts are always doomed to failure. Only a tentative plan is possible, because the universe may change as a result of man's use of his freedom and his creative power.

Furthermore, the sinfulness of man means that his reasoning power does not provide eternal truths. Instead the corrupting influence of self-interest may lead him to develop plans which he believes have a universal value, but which in fact are only a reflection of his own values which are shaped by self-interest. Therefore, it is impossible for man to devise the ideal plan which is consistent with all that is good. One man has the power and the freedom to act in a way which will disrupt the most carefully reasoned plans of another man even when both are motivated by what each perceives to be the highest good.

One can find planners from each of these two schools in almost any gathering. The Aquinas adherents are arguing for the adoption of a carefully prepared, beautifully drawn, thoroughly documented master plan which, it is promised, will provide impartial and objective answers to all the questions that plague the community.

The planners who are in harmony with Niebuhr will deny the feasibility of the master-plan concept and protest that no planner has either the wisdom or the objectivity necessary for the preparation of such a master plan as is proposed by the Aquinas school. They may agree to the adoption of a tentative plan, perhaps in the form of a series of policy statements; however, they would insist that these statements must be continuously open for revision and that frequently it will be necessary and proper to develop a compromise solution to many of the planning problems which are laid before the decision makers.

Quite obviously most planners will not find themselves in unreserved agreement with either of the two positions outlined in this illustration. But an examination of the ideas of Niebuhr and other theologians will enable the planner to clarify and systematize his own concepts of the planning process. Today, as perhaps never before, many theologians apparently are ready and eager to help him to do this.

The third contribution that the theologians have made is in helping the planner to understand himself, his role, and his relationship to other men and to institutions such as the church and the government, and to God.

The focal point of this contribution is the theologian's emphasis on the values and norms which are central to the decision-making process. Christian social ethics is the particular branch of theology which is specifically concerned with an analysis of decision making. An illustration of the contribution a theologian can make in this area is that he may help the planner realize that there is an inherent moral compulsion resting on him to try to offer to the decision makers alternate courses of action in a manner which will enable the people to have a really free choice and to comprehend the probable consequences of each alternative. If the planner can comprehend and respond to this requirement it will help him to avoid the common dilemma of many planners—that of attempting to defend a single recommendation rather than interpreting a variety of alternatives and the probable consequences of each.

This moral compulsion or sense of "oughtness" is a part of the makeup of every person. It is countered, however, by the innate freedom which man possesses. The freedom needs a guide, and the compulsion requires an explanation. Today's planner is a living example of Berdyaev's contention that man is now more eager than ever before for freedom, the exercise of compassion, and the chance to be creative.[6] The Judeo-Christian ethic offers the planner an explanation of these forces which constrain him first to choose planning as a vocation and second to be motivated by an unending search for the good. Both the motivation and the guidance for this search can be found in a study of Judeo-Christian ethics. When this becomes real "it becomes impulse and energy and inspiration." [7]

If the planner is acquainted with the writings of E. S. Brightman he will understand the importance of consistency and coherence and be able to see that in many respects planning is a search for coherence. The value of a systematic frame of reference is as great for the planner as for the theo-

[6] Nicholas Berdyaev, *The Destiny of Man* (New York: Charles Scribner's Sons, 1937), pp. 197-204.

[7] William Temple, *Nature, Man and God* (London: Macmillan & Company, Ltd., 1956), p. 381.

logian. Neither can operate effectively from a base comprised of a handful of hackneyed moralisms.

The planner, like few other people in our society, is subject to a tremendous temptation to play at being God. The theologian's warning that both he and the planning goals which he proposes are under God's judgment may reduce the attractiveness of this temptation. The theologian's emphasis on the "I-Thou" relationship may help the planner resist the temptation to try to manipulate people and to regard other persons as things rather than as the unique creations of God.

The planner who is also a practicing theologian will be better able to comprehend the conflicts which are inherent in planning. He will be able to understand why he often finds himself in a position of tension between his clientele and the rest of the world. He will be able to distinguish between the pressures of institutional survival and the call to service. He will be prepared to help the decision makers formulate goals which are consistent with the basic purpose of the organization rather than adopt goals which are motivated out of a spirit of self-interest or a desire for bureaucratic glory.

The planner-theologian will be able to see why the goals of city planners and of churchmen so often are in conflict. Sometimes this conflict may result from the institutional pressures on the city planner which cause him to assign greater importance to things such as cars and buildings than to persons. It happens with surprising frequency, however, that this conflict grows out of a theological misunderstanding of the church. The city planner may view the local church as a religious institution seeking to minister to the spiritual needs of the nearby residents. The clergyman may act from an institutional perspective which places the major emphasis on perpetuating the life of the institution. An all too common illustration of this is the decision to leave a Protestant church building standing in the middle of an urban renewal area in which all other buildings are to be razed and replaced with new apartment towers. The planner agrees to this arrangement because he sees the church as a positive force in building a sense of community among the new residents of the renewal area. The pastor and members of the church agree because they want to preserve the life of their institution. The common result is that the church building is left standing on condition that it be repaired and remodeled so that it complies with the city building code; in the relocation process the nearby members of the church move to another part of the city; the church (because of the institutional pressure to maintain itself) ministers to these absentee members and ignores the newcomers who move into the apartments next door. The renewal planner sees what happens, is disillusioned, and in planning the next renewal project makes no special allowance for leaving existing churches in the area. Therefore, the pastor and trustees of a church which would like to remain become embroiled in a conflict with the city over the municipality's right to buy the property of a congregation which does not wish to move. The contributions of the theologian will not eliminate these conflicts, but it will help both parties understand the causes of the conflict and thus may help in resolving the differences.

These three areas in which theologians have contributed to the planner's understanding of his role and place do not begin to exhaust the possibilities, but they do illustrate the relevant resources which the theologian can bring into the conversation that always is a part of courtship. They also indicate that the responsibility for turning this courtship into a marriage rests primarily on the planner. The theologians have made the initial overture. It is now up to the planners to respond.

4

Interdenominational Church Planning
+++

DURING THE PAST DOZEN YEARS INTERDENOMINATIONAL
church planning offices with full-time professional staff members have been established in Detroit, Indianapolis, St.
Louis, the District of Columbia, Chicago, Philadelphia,
Cleveland-Akron, Buffalo, and in several state councils of
churches. In some instances the work is administered and
financed directly by the local council of churches. In others
the financial support comes directly from the denominations
and the administrative responsibility is vested in a committee
composed of denominational representatives.

Agencies such as these represent the latest development
in the history of cooperative church planning which began
in the latter part of the nineteenth century and went under
the name of "comity." [1] Knowledge of the development of

---

[1] An earlier bilateral effort at interdenominational church planning was
the famous "Plan of Union," an arrangement approved in 1801 between

comity, its advantages, its short-comings, and its contributions, is necessary for anyone seeking to understand the forces
which have shaped contemporary efforts in cooperative
church planning.

The word "comity" did not come into the vocabulary of
Protestant churchmen until several decades after the practice
had been widely accepted in the foreign mission field. Almost from its very beginnings the Protestant foreign missionary efforts were characterized by a sense of interdenominational cooperation. Before long informal arrangements were
being made by which the missionaries agreed on a geographical division of responsibilities which would prevent un-
economical duplication of effort. Perhaps the first such informal agreement was the one made in 1830 between two
missionaries representing the London Missionary Society and
two Wesleyan Methodists in the South Pacific. They agreed
that the Tonga and Fiji Islands would be occupied by the
Methodists and Samoa by the L. M. S.[2]

Such agreements became widespread in the foreign field
and were possible only because of the sense of Christian
unity which overcame national and denominational barriers.
Without this sense of unity comity would never have come
into being, and without this sense of unity comity is doomed.

As this spirit of cooperation grew the definition of comity
was sharpened and included three distinct elements: (1)
The assignment of a specific geographical area to one church
body, (2) positive respect for the work, achievements, and

the Connecticut Association of the Congregational Church and the General
Assembly of the Presbyterian Church, by which the two denominations
agreed to cooperate in organizing new churches in the West. The Congregationalists terminated the agreement in 1850, although its influence lingered
on for over a century. See Gaius G. Atkins and Frederick L. Fagley, *History
of American Congregationalism* (Boston: Pilgrim Press, 1942), pp. 142-48,
195-98, 343-44 and 400.

[2] R. Pierce Beaver, *Ecumenical Beginnings in Protestant World Mission*
(New York: Thomas Nelson & Sons, 1962), pp. 44-45.

standards of other denominations, and (3) recognition of the fact that the task of evangelizing the world was larger than the resources of any single Protestant church body.

The idea of comity in foreign missions was widely accepted and practiced by the middle of the nineteenth century, but it was not until 1888 that the word itself came into popular usage. In that year the Centenary Conference of Protestant Missions of the World was held in London, and papers were presented on the need for mutual agreements in the delineation of territory for missionary activities. Both in the papers and in the ensuing discussions the word "comity" was used repeatedly.[3] Acceptance of the term followed acceptance of the practice by more than a half century.

The Rise of Comity in America

It was at about this same time that the idea of comity entered the scene in America. The idea was sparked by a series of articles which Washington Gladden, a famous Congregational minister in Hartford, Connecticut, wrote for *The Century Magazine* in 1882 and 1883.

In these entertaining articles, which took the form of reports from "The Christian League of Connecticut," Gladden made a fervent and well-reasoned plea for cooperation rather than competition and conflict. The "League" was formed "to promote efficiency and economy in Christian work, by the suppression and extinction of superfluous organizations, by the occupation of destitute fields, and by the concentration of Christian people."

There was a special emphasis in the articles on the problems of overchurching small towns, and Gladden suggested one church for every 500 persons as an appropriate ratio. One of the "members" of the "League" is quoted as saying,

[3] *Ibid.,* pp. 66-71.

"I go in for hanging every man that proposes the second church in a town of less than five hundred people." [4]

Gladden's suggestions included three concepts that have constituted a basis for most comity agreements. (1) Denominational labels are of little importance, and any church should be able to minister to all residents of an area. (2) Church bodies collectively should be able to wield sufficient authority to regulate the number of churches that will be operating in a given area. (3) Protestantism can serve more efficiently and effectively in a community if represented by a few medium- and large-size congregations rather than by many small ones; thus it is better to have three churches, each with 400 members, than ten churches, each with 120 members.

Gladden was an idealist in many ways and his *Century* articles are typical of that idealism. Gladden's idealism was infectious, and his articles led to a meeting of denominational officials to discuss the possibilities of instituting comity arrangements in New England. The first meeting was held in Brunswick, Maine, in 1890, and a year later delegates from several Protestant denominations met and adopted a statement of principles.[5] This pioneering effort became the model for most subsequent comity agreements.

The concept of comity spread rapidly over the Northeastern and North-central parts of the country but made very little impact in the South. Denominations such as the Presbyterians, Methodists (especially the Methodist Protestant Church), Congregationalists, and Evangelicals were strong supporters of comity. The Lutherans and the Episcopalians

[4] Washington Gladden, "The Christian League of Connecticut," *The Century Magazine* (November, 1882), pp. 50-60 (December, 1882), pp. 181-91 (January, 1883), pp. 339-49 (May, 1883), pp. 65-79.

[5] Charles S. MacFarland, *Christian Unity in Practice and Prophecy* (New York: The Macmillan Company, 1933), p. 129.

were more reluctant to enter into comity arrangements and often did not participate at all.

Frequently the desire to organize a comity committee pre-ceeded and stimulated the desire for organization of a local federation of churches, and comity was one of the major functions of state and local councils of churches.[6]

The underlying principles of comity changed little during the first few decades of its life. The seven principles which were adopted in Maine in 1891 reveal the goals that the founders of comity had in mind.

1. No denomination should enter a community in which another denomination has a legitimate claim without first conferring with the denominations having such claims.

2. Whenever possible a feeble church should be revived rather than a new one of a rival denomination organized.

3. If other factors are equal the denomination having churches nearest a particular community should have first claim on organizing a new church in that community.

4. The preferences of the community should be a factor in deciding which denomination shall go in, however.

5. There should be no interference with a denomination which has initiated a new work in a community.

6. Temporary suspension of work by a denomination is not sufficient justification for the entrance of other denominations.

7. The Comity Commission shall decide questions of interpretation of these principles.[7]

Ideas and phrases similar to these can be found in the wording of comity principles adopted in other parts of the

[6] H. Paul Douglass, *Church Comity* (New York: Institute of Social and Religious Research, 1929), pp. 2-29.

[7] These statements are condensed from the "Seven Principles" which are quoted in full in Roy B. Guild, editor, *The Manual of Inter-Church Work* (New York: The Federal Council of the Churches of Christ in America, 1917), p. 18.

nation. The emphasis was clearly on cooperative action which would minimize interference by one denomination with the work of others. Quite simply the central goal was to avoid "overlooking" and "overlapping." [8]

As the comity operation became institutionalized two significant trends emerged. One was the centralization of decision making within the comity committee with the result that it sought to be able to exercise an effective control over the actions of the participating denominations. The second was the attempt to develop standard operating procedures and principles which, it was hoped, would result in an objective guide for the making of difficult decisions.

As these two trends developed the nature of comity changed. It changed from a vague concept of noninterference and cooperation to a rather rigid plan which would prevent competition. If the comity committees of the 1911-42 period had been subject to the Sherman anti-trust laws it is doubtful if any could have survived their day in court!

The One-Mile Rule

Perhaps the most striking, and certainly the most controversial example of this was the widespread adoption of the "one-mile rule." This was—and still is—one of the common criteria used in determining the number and location of new churches. The usual interpretation of this restriction is that a new "comity" church should not be located within one mile of any existing or proposed church which is related to a denomination sharing in the comity agreement.

It is interesting to note that H. Paul Douglass, the most distinguished name in the history of the comity movement, objected to this concept and argued that "comity should therefore concern itself with grouping, rather than with the

---

[8] Douglass, *op. cit.,* p. 8.

exclusive attempt to spread the churches out as far as possible from one another." [9]

An evaluation of the one-mile rule reveals the fallacies inherent in the assumptions on which it rests, the adverse conditions which may result in a rigid application of the rule, and some of the problems inherent in the comity procedures.

Proponents of the one-mile rule offer a variety of justifications for its use. A brief examination of the ten most common assumptions on which the one-mile rule is predicated will reveal why it is more often a source of tension than a useful tool in resolving differences of opinion.

1. *All denominations sharing in comity arrangements are sufficiently similar that each can serve all Protestants in a given area.* In fact, one observes that there are major differences among the various denominations—in theology, in the sacraments, in definition of church membership, in the concept of the church, in social action, in the concept of the ministry, et cetera. These differences are real; they are important; and many laymen are aware of them.

2. *The appropriate service radius for a church is one mile, and therefore, churches should be one mile apart.* The few sound studies that have been completed indicate that a one-half mile radius is a more appropriate distance and is as far as a church can reach before factors other than distance become primary considerations.

3. *The church's parish can be defined in geographical terms.* Historically this has been the case and still is true for Roman Catholicism, Orthodox Judaism, some newly organized churches, and many rural churches. For most urban churches, however, the parish can be described more accurately in nongeographical (social class, denomination,

[9] *Ibid.,* p. 145.

ethnic background, income, vocation, age, et cetera) rather than in geographical terms.

4. *The geographical relationship to other Protestant churches is the primary consideration in locating new churches.* Perhaps it is far more important to be near the center of the community, to be at a highly accessible location, to be on a desirable site, and to be near public transportation.

5. *The word "church" has certain universal qualities in regard to size.* The emphasis on the distance factor tends to suggest that all churches are the same. How far apart should 300-member churches be? How close should 2,000-member churches be to one another? Some congregations want to be small; some hope to be large. The one-mile rule tends to overlook this factor.

6. *Physical distance is the best single objective measurement in locating new churches.* A better objective measurement is density of population. In an area with a population density of one hundred persons per acre it may be desirable to have churches across the street from one another. In areas with a density of one or two persons per acre it may be desirable to have churches two, three, or five miles apart.

7. *It is desirable for most of the people in one neighborhood to be served by the same church.* While it may be convenient for a local church to have all its members living near the church and to have all the nearby residents as members, this is a far different value-judgment than to suggest that a local church is entitled to either a monopoly or a prior claim on the religious affiliations of residents of a particular geographical area. Many Protestants today favor religious diversity and would be as opposed to the artificial creation of a religious ghetto as they would be to the creation of a racial ghetto.

8. *The one-mile rule implies that many of the criteria*

used in planning public schools are appropriate for locating Protestant churches. The fallacies in this assumption should be obvious to anyone who supports both equality of educational opportunity and the right of diversity of religious belief.

9. *The one-mile distance is a universal and objective yardstick.* It ignores the number of denominations sharing in comity arrangements; it ignores population density; it ignores the religious characteristics of the population.

10. *Protestantism should offer a single ecumenical outreach in each neighborhood.* Even if one grants that this is desirable it is contradicted by history, which indicates that Protestantism is able to have a universal appeal only through a splintered approach. Furthermore, many comity committees supported the principle of "self-determination," the idea that the religious preferences of the residents would determine the denominational label of the church that would be organized in the area. Such a sectarian approach is inconsistent with the concept of a single ecumenical mission. If 40 per cent of the residents of an area are Baptists, does this mean that the 35 per cent who may be Episcopalians cannot have their own church? Which principle is more important, an ecumenical outreach or the freedom of self-determination? Does the principle of an ecumenical outreach mean that the minority right of self-determination must yield to majority (or more often plurality) rule?

What are the effects of the one-mile rule when it is used by a comity committee?

1. It frequently leads to the acquisition of a second-rate site, chosen not because of the needs of the new congregation, but because of the prior decision of an existing congregation which probably did not take into consideration the location of future churches when it chose its own site.

2. Application of the one-mile rule inhibits the freedom

of cooperating denominations, often leaving the most desirable and logical sites for use by noncooperating denominations.

3. Application of the one-mile rule sets up unnecessary geographical barriers which separate and isolate local churches. Frequently it may mean that churches which would cooperate and present a united Protestant witness cannot do this because of geographical separation. This is particularly a problem in suburban areas where the fragmentation of local government is a major consideration. Thus a new church may have to be in a different municipality in order to be a mile from other churches. This inhibits united action and presents an image of isolation and noncooperation.

4. The dispersal of local churches is in direct contradiction to the efforts of community planners who are seeking to facilitate the development of a focus for community life. Many planners would prefer to see three, four, or five churches clustered in or near the geographical focus of community life rather than to have them scattered in a pattern similar to the location of fire stations.

5. The one-mile rule does not permit the establishment of an adequate number of churches. Strict application of the one-mile radius often will result in underchurching a metropolitan area. For example, if this standard had been applied to Hamilton County (Greater Cincinnati) the ceiling on Protestantism would be 414 churches—and more than one half of these would be in highly unsuitable areas (the flood plain, on slopes with a grade of 20 per cent or more, in industrial areas, et cetera). Fourteen "white" Protestant denominations have over 300 local congregations in Hamilton County today, and there are probably that many additional Protestant congregations among the other Protestant denominations. While some may argue that it is undesirable

to have so many churches, it nevertheless appears that in most metropolitan areas there will be one church for every 800 to 1,200 residents. Should evangelical Protestantism limit itself by a rigid geographical quota?

The one-mile rule illustrates some of the shortcomings which were inherent in comity, but there also were other weaknesses which contributed to its eventual decline. Before discussing these in detail, however, the positive contributions of comity should be reviewed.

While many old-time supporters of comity may be reluctant to admit it, comity has failed to meet the needs of Protestantism during the post World War II suburban church building boom. This does not mean, however, that comity made no positive contributions to the work of American Protestantism since its inception nearly seventy-five years ago.

Perhaps its greatest contribution was that it provided an arena in which denominational representatives could come together and wrestle with the problems of "churching" America. A channel of communication was established for the exchange of ideas, goals, and procedures, Sometimes the communication was impeded by disruptive static, but there was communication.

Second, comity helped denominational executives and local churchmen see themselves and their efforts as a part of the universal church. This was as important in its spiritual impact as it was in its institutional effect.

A third contribution was that in many communities comity arrangements did reduce duplication and overlapping of effort, and also called attention to neglected and overlooked fields.

Finally, comity helped to establish a climate of cooperation which has had a favorable influence not only on subsequent developments in interchurch planning, but also on a variety of other interdenominational activities including the development of local councils of churches.

The Decline of Comity

While it would be a gross exaggeration to say that comity ever gained the approval in home-mission activities that it enjoyed in the foreign field, it did achieve a wide measure of acceptance in many Northern cities for several decades. When put to its greatest test, however—the suburban church building boom of 1946-61—comity failed to provide a workable procedure for coordinating Protestant efforts. In city after city meetings of the local comity committee became the scene of bewilderment, belligerence, bickering, and back scratching. Rivalry often supplanted unity as the dominant spirit. Denominationalism replaced cooperativeness as the basis for decision making. Stalemate replaced agreement as the fruit of such meetings.

A number of explanations can be offered for the failure of comity at this critical point in the history of home missions. Some of the blame must be assigned to the inadequacies of the comity committees and some to the nature of American Protestantism.

All too many comity committees included members who did not have a direct voice in the decision-making processes of their own denominations. Frequently a denomination would be represented in a local comity committee by the pastor of a local church while the actual decisions were being made, perhaps in another city, by full-time denominational officials charged with the responsibility for new church development. Not infrequently this meant either (1) that the pastor serving on the comity committee was without real power to speak for his denomination, or (2) that he was asked to bring in for ratification by the comity committee a decision that had already been made by persons in the hierarchy of his denomination.

Furthermore, in all but a few instances the comity committee did not have adequate factual information on which it could make intelligent decisions. They did not have the assistance of professional staff persons who could systematically assemble and interpret the available data. A map, a ruler, a few population statistics, and perhaps the results of an amateur religious census or a windshield survey of the area constituted most, if not all, of the resources available to the committee.

A third weakness of comity was that it was not inclusive. Normally the committee included representatives from only those denominations which in that community were "cooperative." This might be as few as five or six and rarely was more than a dozen. In almost every metropolitan center, however, many other church groups were busy organizing new churches in suburbia. Thus on Tuesday the committee might reject the request of the Congregationalists to acquire a new church site at the corner of University Avenue and State Road because it was too close to the Presbyterian and Methodist churches, only to read in Sunday's newspaper that a non-cooperative denomination had purchased a site even closer to the Presbyterian and Methodist churches! What price cooperation?

This lack of inclusiveness had other facets. Comity not only did not include the denominations which were not interested in participating in ecumenical endeavors—but which were interested in establishing new churches—it usually did not have a place for representatives from cooperative-minded community churches and only rarely included representatives from Negro churches. A survey by H. Paul Douglass found only one Negro among the 318

members of the comity committees responding to his ques-
tionnaire.[10]

Another of the most important of the inherent weaknesses
of the usual comity committee was the reliance on inadequate standards. The controversial one-mile rule is but one
example of this. In allocating new church sites should each
denomination receive one, or should the distribution be in
proportion to the size of the denominations? The large denominations objected to the former because it restricted
their efforts to continue to grow at their former pace, and
the small denominations objected to the latter because it
prevented them from enlarging their local strength. Another
example of the inadequacy of standards with its resulting
conflicts involved measurement of growth and purpose.
Should growth be measured in terms of new housing units,
in terms of additional residents, or in terms of the number
of newcomers of a particular religious preference? Were new
churches being planned to serve primarily the persons with
a certain religious preference or to be evangelical in bringing
the gospel to everyone? Rarely was a local comity committee
able to develop satisfactory answers to questions such as these.

The practice of comity also was hampered by the nature
of American Protestantism. Regardless of alleged polity, most
self-supporting local churches enjoy a high degree of congregational autonomy, and this impeded comity efforts. Part
of the suburban population boom was the result of the
exodus of many residents from the central city. Frequently
people from the same neighborhood moved to the same general section of suburbia, and it was only natural that they
would try to take their churches with them. Sometimes the
spirit of cooperation was sufficiently strong that the congrega-

---

[10] *Ibid.*, p. 67. For a case study of the limitations of comity in one city
see Philip M. Smith, "Protestant Comity in Metropolitan Pittsburgh,"
American Sociological Review, vol. 8, pp. 425-32.

tion sought, and waited for, approval of the appropriate denominational and interdenominational committees. All too often the congregations merely announced their decision and proceeded to implement it without waiting for anyone's approval. When a local church in a "cooperating" denomination chose this latter course of action it not only complicated the comity operation, it also embarrassed the participants.

This same element of congregational autonomy also had an adverse effect on comity in those communities where an essential part of the practice was to hold "hearings" on each proposal for the establishment of a new church. The usual procedure was to invite the pastors of all of the cooperating local churches in the area to attend and to comment on the proposal. This had the obvious advantage of bringing into the decision-making process the special knowledge which these pastors had of the area. But this also brought a new voice and a quite different perspective into the scene. Generally the members of a comity committee favored the idea of new church development or they would not be serving on such a voluntary committee. By contrast most pastors were reluctant to see additional "competition" in their own community.

For example, the pastor of one local church objected to the establishment of any new congregations in his community on the grounds that his church had not reached its full growth. When asked how many persons were members of his church he replied, "Twenty-two hundred." It was not at all unusual to see the pastor of a local church opposing the position taken by his denominational representative on the comity committee. Such intradenominational differences did not ease the tensions inherent in comity.

Perhaps the crucial flaw in the comity concept is an outgrowth of the nature of the decision-making process in voluntary associations which are working with autonomous agencies.

The comity committee was a voluntary association seeking to control decisions which would be implemented on a unilateral basis by the individual churches or denominations. Like most voluntary associations it found that the power of veto was easier to wield than the power of initiation and implementation. Unlike many other voluntary associations, however, the comity committee actually possessed very little power. A taxpayers' alliance can be formed, and while it rarely can force positive action, it often can exercise an effective minority veto and defeat a referendum for a bond issue or a tax levy. The comity committee had no similar power. It had no sanctions. If a denomination or local church ignored the decision of the comity committee there was no way of "punishing" such action. Comity depended solely upon a "cooperative spirit." Such a spirit is often the only motivation needed for progressive action, but it is of limited value in enforcing a veto. Wartime alliances can be built on the spirit of cooperation, but peacetime disarmament proposals (which are "veto-type" actions) require some form of enforcement. Comity was caught in this dilemma. It is the nature of most voluntary associations to drift in the direction of vetoing proposals rather than initiating new plans for action. Comity drifted in this direction, but had no power to enforce its veto.

As a result of these factors time after time comity committees were forced to choose between reluctantly ratifying a decision which they did not approve and exercising a veto which could not be enforced.

At this critical point many comity committees, instead of attempting to develop a program which would offer a more positive approach to the reconciliation of differences, moved instead to develop means of enforcing its veto. Thus in many communities the comity agreement was rewritten to include words which had the ring of compulsion; i.e., "allocation," "authorization," "assignment," and "appeal." Gradually the decision makers in the various denominations came to view comity, not as a device for cooperative planning, but rather as an obstacle which must be hurdled before they could implement their own denominational program. When comity moved from cooperation to coercion it signed its own death warrant.

Finally comity suffered because of its very limited scope. Comity was "growth" oriented, and most of the procedures were developed to cover growth situations, particularly the growth of the metropolitan areas with the concomitant need for additional new Protestant churches on the periphery of the central city.

During the past three decades, however, and particularly since the end of World War II, it has become apparent that the heart of the church planning problem is not one of "growth" but of "change." The growth of suburbia is but one facet of the total picture of change which challenges Protestantism in both urban and rural America.

Comity committees were oriented toward coordinating the location of new suburban churches, but they had little to offer in the way of assistance in cooperative planning for the retreat from the central city or for coping with the changes wrought by urban renewal, chronic unemployment, or expressway construction. As more assistance was needed than comity could supply, the decision makers of Protestantism sought new approaches to the subject of interdenominational church planning.

Research and Planning

The failure of comity to meet the needs of cooperative Protestant groups in an expanding urban America resulted in a twofold move in a different direction. One result of this new thinking was to wipe out the memory of unpleasant past experiences by changing the name of the game. Instead of "comity," the committee concerned with cooperative church extension was given a new title—Interchurch Relations, or Planning and Strategy, or Research and Planning. In too many cities it continued to be the same old game, however— one denominational executive referred to it as "the place where they hand out hunting licenses."

The second forward-looking step was to engage professional staff assistance for the comity committee—or its successor. Such action recognized that one of the causes for the failure of comity was that decisions were being made on the basis of inadequate information. Obviously the way to correct this would be to engage a person on either a full- or part-time basis who would be responsible for gathering and interpreting relevant data. While it was somewhat presumptuous to dignify this function with the term "research," this word frequently was used. Since the information was to be used for planning new church locations, it appeared logical to designate the new committee the "research and planning" committee or department of the local council of churches. Frequently this change in name was made, but without the addition of staff.

Thus during the dozen or so years following the end of World War II the concept of comity was being replaced by the somewhat more positive idea of a research and planning agency which would be a part of the state or local council of churches.

In addition, many denominations established research and planning or research and survey departments within the framework of the denominational organization. Sometimes these were a part of a regional administrative agency, but more often they were a department within the national board of home missions. Frequently these denominational agencies were able to attract extremely well-qualified and competent personnel as staff members. Often they would go out and work with local denominational officials in studying an area and making recommendations on new church developments. These recommendations would then be forwarded to the local comity committee for consideration.

By now Protestantism has had enough experience with the research and planning concept that it can be evaluated. Most observers agree that it does represent real progress over the older comity idea but the degree of progress varies greatly. In appraising the efforts thus far a distinction must be made between denominational and interdenominational efforts.

On the denominational level the major emphasis has been to establish an office in the national board of home missions. Basically these offices tend to emphasize survey work, and in general most of the work is of superior quality. Frequently these surveys follow the same general format of "the local church and its immediate neighborhood" and are focused either on a single congregation or on all the congregations of that denomination in a city, a county, a district, a diocese, or a conference.

While these denominational surveys can be valuable tools for a congregation or for the regional office of a denomination in its planning, they possess both advantages and disadvantages. There are three major advantages. The first is the benefit of direction and interpretation by a trained, experienced, and objective outsider who has no axes to grind nor skeletons to hide. A second advantage is the accumulation of knowledge and wisdom which accrues to a denomination and its staff as they direct these surveys throughout the church. Because these are carried out on a denominational basis it is possible to develop and use a consistent procedure which will enable the denominational officials to gain a clearer view of reality as the data from a large number of surveys are accumulated. Finally, the denominational office often is in a unique position to carry on special research projects which are valuable in the development of denomination-wide programs. Such a department can be a valuable staff arm to the operating (line) departments of the board of home missions.

The disadvantages become more apparent as an increasingly large number of denominations carry on such programs. Perhaps the most obvious disadvantage is the duplication of effort as each denomination sends men out to make a unilateral analysis of a particular community. For example, in the three years immediately preceding the establishment of the Regional Church Planning Office in Cleveland, Ohio, four separate denominations had staff persons visiting that city to direct or carry out denominational surveys. A second disadvantage is that the denominational survey tends to accentuate denominational lines. Such a study reports only what a part of the universal church is doing in that community. The Methodist survey, for example, largely ignores the ministry of the Lutherans, the Presbyterians, and the Episcopalians, and rarely does anyone even begin to measure the impact of the sects and the noncooperative denominations.

The most important disadvantage is the difficulty of effective implementation and "follow-through." Local church surveys by visiting experts are subject to the same shortcomings that handicap use of the master plans prepared for cities by consultants. Most cities now recognize that while a consultant may make valuable contributions, it is even more important for the city to have the benefit of continuing assistance from a resident planner. There is a strong parallel in local church planning. One result is that some denominations are now adding research and planning men to the regional staff. For example, the first person called by the United Church of Christ in Ohio was a full-time minister in charge of research and planning for the denomination in that state.

If the research and planning office is located in the state or local council of churches, it substantially reduces the impact of these two disadvantages.[11] This procedure has disadvantages, however.

The most important disadvantage is that any planning effort which is outside the denominational structure tends to be isolated from the locus of decision making. This is especially a problem in those councils which are councils of *local* churches and which do not provide adequate opportunity for *denominational* representation in the research and planning department. This is the same disadvantage which hampered comity.

A second problem is geography. Most Protestant denominations are moving toward increasing the authority of the regional office. Frequently this area is larger than that covered by the metropolitan council of churches but smaller than the jurisdiction of the state council of churches. In urban regions, which are replacing the metropolitan areas as the contemporary form of urbanism, the limited jurisdiction of the local council of churches severely handicaps the research and planning department. On the other hand, in states such as Ohio, Texas, New York, and California, each of which contains several urban regions, the territory covered by the state council of churches is far too large and heterogeneous to enable a state council research and planning de-

---

[11] A brief history of the interdenominational research and planning movement is offered by Walter Kloetzli, "The History and Present Situation in Research and Planning," *Search* (New York: National Council of Churches, 1960), p. 20.

partment to have more than limited relevance or effectiveness.

New Structures

These limitations and disadvantages have forced Protestant leaders to seek new structures which would combine the advantages of a cooperative approach with an elimination of the disadvantages which have plagued comity and other interdenominational procedures.

One proposal which is receiving increasing attention is based on two assumptions that appear to be valid. The first is that the urban region, rather than the state or the metropolitan area, is the logical basis for planning.[12] This idea has already been recognized and accepted by many public planners concerned with such functions as water resources and transportation. It has been recognized by businessmen in such functions as banking, retailing, wholesaling, and insurance. More recently many churchmen are seeing the value and usefulness of this concept in structuring the administrative organization of a denomination. The best examples can be seen in the structures resulting when two or three denominations merge.

The second assumption is that the denominations are legitimate orders of creation and that their efforts, decisions, and actions are to be respected. This concept is totally rejected by some churchmen who view the denominations as roadblocks in the path to church union and who believe the *proper* place for Protestant decision making is within interdenominational councils. Without getting into the theological merits of this argument, one important observation can and must be made. In contemporary Protestantism most

---

[12] For an analysis of the emergence of the urban region see Lyle E. Schaller, "The Urban Region: The Successor to the City and the Metropolitan Area?" *Mayor and Manager* (April, 1963), pp. 10-17.

important decisions *are* made and implemented within the structures of each of the several denominations and *not* by interdenominational agencies.

On the basis of these two assumptions it has been proposed that an effective structure for interdenominational church planning can be established which includes an entire urban region and which relates directly to the regional offices of the several participating denominations. Such a structure solves the problem of geographical jurisdiction by including a natural economic and social area rather than being tied to the political boundaries of a city or state. Thus in Buffalo the Buffalo-Niagara Falls urban region provides a natural planning region, as does the Cleveland-Akron-Lorain-Elyria region in northeastern Ohio or the Cincinnati-Hamilton-Dayton region in southwestern Ohio. This concept gives a flexibility which is highly desirable in this urban age.

If one office can be made to serve a number of denominations within a single region much of the duplication of effort in research and survey which characterizes the denominational approach can be avoided. One interdenominational agency can gather information, interpret data, and serve as a liaison with secular agencies almost as effectively and at much less expense than could several denominational planning agencies.[13]

The final, and perhaps the most important point is the emphasis which this concept places on a direct relationship between the church planner and the denominational decision makers. Relating the interdenominational planning

[13] For a constructive apologetic from another viewpoint of inter-denominational church planning on a regional basis see H. Conrad Hoyer, "Creative Interdenominational Planning for Church Extension," an address delivered to the Interdenominational Consultation on Church Extension held at Valley Forge, Pa., February 20-21, 1963, and available in mimeographed form from the Division of Home Missions of the National Council of the Churches of Christ in the U.S.A.

agency directly to the regional office of the denominations provides the greatest opportunity for the church planner to serve effectively as a staff aid to the people who today are making and implementing the decisions which will shape the Protestantism of tomorrow. This relationship also avoids many of the frustrating and embarrassing situations which may arise when an interdenominational agency works directly with local churches rather than through the appropriate denominational channels. Most denominations, including those which allegedly operate on some form of congregational polity, have rather clear-cut intradenominational channels of communication. The church planner can be most effective if he works through these channels rather than through new ones. This structure enhances the possibility that the interdenominational staff planner will be able to work with the appropriate decision makers.

In a structure such as this the interdenominational church planner has a clearly defined relationship as a staff adviser to denominational and local church groups. In addition, he also has an important role as a communicator. The vertical organization of institutional Protestantism means that the channels of communication connecting the local church, the regional office, and the national boards usually are superior to those cutting across denominational lines at any level of the organization. Therefore, one of the most valuable contributions that an interdenominational church planning office can make is to provide this horizontal channel of communication at the regional level. In part this can be accomplished through the creation of an interdenominational planning committee; in part it must be accomplished by the staff planner who has established a direct relationship with the decision makers in each of several denominations and, therefore, is in a position to serve as a communicator across denominational lines.

Today's concept of interdenominational church planning varies substantially from the dream that Washington Gladden had over eighty years ago, but there are many similarities. Both are premised on the desirability of preventing needless duplication of effort and costly competition for members. Both recognize the imperative to think in terms of service rather than of institutional growth. Both are based on the realistic understanding that no single church body has the resources, the wisdom, and the strength necessary to meet single-handedly all the new church needs in America.

Perhaps the major difference between Gladden's dream of cooperative church extension and today's concept of church planning is the current pragmatic recognition of the importance of two "isms"—urbanism and denominationalism.

5

Church Planning Principles
+++

The city fathers of Elmtown were getting a number of complaints about the traffic congestion on Main Street. During the evening rush hours it was almost impossible to drive through town. At any moment an observer could see pedestrians darting across the street in mid-block and automobiles pulling in or out of curbside parking spaces, turning off to the side streets, and double-parking to pick up or let off passengers. In addition to the undisciplined habits of both drivers and pedestrians, there also were many people who used Main Street to get from their homes on one side of town to their places of work on the other side and back home again. Inasmuch as the stores and office buildings on Main Street were built right up to the property lines, it was obvious that the street could not be widened except at a prohibitive cost.

Finally the mayor sought and gained permission from the

city council to call in a planning consultant to study the problem—although several councilmen were positive that any
solution that an outside expert could propose would be far
too expensive for the city's limited budget.

The traffic consultant was hired, however, and after studying the situation for an hour he went back to City Hall,
and with the help of some maps, prepared a six-point program that was easily within the financial limitations of the
community. *He was able to do this because he understood
several basic planning principles.* The consultant knew that
the congestion could be reduced by painting lane stripes on
the pavement, by prohibiting left turns at several intersections and providing left-turn lanes at those points where
turns were permitted, by synchronizing the traffic signals to
accommodate the direction of heavier traffic volume, by
painting pedestrian walk lanes at the intersections, and by
modest physical changes at one intersection which converted
a diagonal street to a right-angle intersection.

The traffic planner has the benefit of many tested basic
planning principles such as these to aid him in planning for
the growth and changes which are occurring in urban America. Unfortunately the church planning profession is still too
new to have developed similar helpful planning principles—
*but it is time that efforts be made to systematize the body
of knowledge we do possess about Protestant churches and to
begin to develop some basic church planning principles.*

Useful church planning principles can only grow out of
research and experience. In every case it will be necessary to
begin with a hypothesis and to test it, refine it, and retest it.
It obviously is true that we may never be able to develop
church-planning principles which will have the same universal application as those used by city planners in dealing with
the physical aspects of urban life, but it is equally true that
churchmen need to use all available knowledge in planning

for the future of Protestantism. Today community planners are behind traffic planners in methodology and skills—and church planners are far behind community planners—but the lag need not be as great as it is.

It must be recognized, however, that the nature of Protestantism, the work of the Holy Spirit, the quality of pastoral leadership, the degree of dedication on the part of the laity, the changing pressures of society, and various theological considerations make church planning a much more subjective area than that within which the city planner is working.

The experiences of many congregations have been used in the formulation of the following basic church planning principles which may be helpful to local churches as they seek to define their own specific purposes and to plan for their future roles. Some of these principles are intended to help a local church understand its relationship to other churches, and some are intended to provide guidance for churches which are confronted with changes in the community, but most have been formulated for use by churches which are seeking to understand themselves. "Know thyself" is a command which applies to churches as well as to churchmen, and few churches will be able to plan for tomorrow unless today they make the effort to understand themselves and the forces which are influencing their actions, programs, and attitudes.

Some of the principles stated here may appear to be so self-evident that the reader will wonder why it is deemed necessary to write them down. Even the most obvious principles often are ignored when churchmen are actually involved in the decision-making process. This paradoxical situation is presented in some detail in the discussion of the first three principles.

1. *It usually is easier to raise money in the local church for a local building program than for any other purpose.*

Nearly every churchman today has been involved, in some way or another, in a local-church building program. As a result of the high mobility of the population plus the unprecedented church building boom of the past dozen years many pastors and laymen have participated in two, three, or more building-fund campaigns. The almost universal experience is that the members will give more generously to the building fund than to either the local operating budget or to missions. It is not unusual for the congregation to contribute in one year to the building fund two or three times the total amount raised by the church in a "normal year." Professional fund raisers often figure that a church can and will contribute an amount (over a period of years) for a building program equal to three to six times the total giving for any one year; however, one seldom hears any expert in church finances suggest that a reasonable goal for a special benevolence project, or for additional staff members, would be more than a fraction of the total annual operating budget.

2. *The amount of money that can be raised, more than any other single factor, determines the size and general character of any major building project.*

Most building programs start when someone has an idea of what the congregation needs in the way of a physical plant. (It is true that occasionally a building program is initiated because someone believes this will be a good "gimmick" to unite a divided congregation, to increase the congregation's interest in the life of the church, or simply to spend some excess cash. Such exceptions are governed even more rigidly by this rule than are the "normal programs," however.) In a newly organized congregation the usual motivation is to have a meeting place of their own. The congregation which already owns a meeting place may want more space, a newer plant, a better or more convenient location, or simply additional facilities.

Very early in the planning it becomes apparent that the financial resources of the congregation will be a decisive consideration. Not infrequently the preliminary estimates of the amount of money which can be raised turn out to be lower than the final financial goal. More often than not, however, this only means that the early calculations were not realistic and that the revised higher figure was the result of a more carefully prepared estimate, and was not due to any increase in the congregation's capacity and willingness to contribute. Perhaps the best supporting evidence for this statement is the experience of professional fund raisers who can come into a local church and very quickly predict with a high degree of accuracy how much money will be pledged in the proposed drive.

3. *It is easier to interest laymen in accepting leadership responsibilities in a building project than in any other aspect of the church's program.*

Obviously this does not apply equally to all church members. Some are dedicated to missions, to Christian education, to evangelism, to social action, or to stewardship cultivation and perhaps will show as much, but no more, interest in a building proposal. In every congregation, however, there are a number of members who are relatively inactive in the ongoing program of the church but who will be willing, and often eager, to work in a building program.

Frequently both the most active members and the pastor are surprised and gratified at the interest and activity shown by some of these previously inactive brethren. This increased tempo of activity is often cited as one of the major fringe benefits of a building program, and as mentioned earlier, sometimes may be one of the justifications for undertaking a particular building effort. No one should be surprised that churches uncover new leaders and workers through a building program, for this is an area in which many of the members have highly relevant skills and experience. This is particularly true of many men who may feel much more at home when reading a blueprint than when reading the Bible, who feel more competent to discuss a balance sheet than the journeys of Paul, and who are less reluctant to ask others to contribute time and money to the building fund than to talk to them about Christ.

One of the natural results of this is that many of these people lapse back into their old pattern of comparative inactivity once the building program is concluded. They do not feel their skills and services are relevant or needed in the regular ongoing program of the church.

These are three of the most obviously self-evident of all basic church planning principles. It is astonishing, however, how few persons recognize either the significance or the consequences of such principles.

The all too common result is that churches have been and are still constructing buildings which will accommodate programs beyond the congregation's financial and leadership capabilities.

If one reflects on the three principles stated earlier, this result appears to be inevitable. If it is easier to raise money for building than for any other purpose, if the quantity of financial resources rather than the actual program of the church is the determining element in deciding on the size of the structure, and if it is easier to secure lay workers for a building campaign than for the regular program of the church, then it should surprise no one to discover that the congregation has less trouble erecting the building than it has using it.

This resulting phenomenon, sometimes called the "post-building blues," is a common occurrence. The usual characteristics are (1) a shortage of funds to meet the operating expenses of the church, which have unexpectedly increased because of new program expenses, higher utility costs, larger insurance premiums, and bigger heating bills, (2) a sudden awareness by some of the leaders, but by few of the other members, that the new church building may require additions to the staff, (3) a shortage of leaders to carry on the expanded program made possible by the new building, and (4) a sense of guilt over having spent so much of the Lord's money on a building when millions of people are starving throughout the world. Sometimes this stirs up a defensive reaction or a feeling that the congregation has a new responsibility which is illustrated by the comment, "Now that we have this new building, we have to justify building it."

The three basic church planning principles which relate to building are perhaps the most obvious and certainly have widespread application, but there are others which are equally helpful although less obvious.

4. *The size and nature of the church plant, more than any other single factor, determine how the pastor will spend his time.*

Recently the chairman of a pulpit committee complained, "Our previous minister did not call on people in their homes the way we thought he should. When he resigned everyone agreed that the new pastor must be a man who liked to call. Finally we found a man who had the reputation of making more home calls each year than any other pastor in the area. We extended a call; he accepted and came to serve as our pastor—but he doesn't do any more calling than his predecessor did! What are we going to do?"

The speaker is an influential member of a 1,200-member congregation which is widely scattered throughout the western half of the metropolis. The church is located a short distance from the center of the city and is housed in a large building which includes an old sanctuary, a large combination gymnasium-fellowship hall, a ten-year-old, sixteen-room

Christian education wing, a small chapel used largely for weddings and funerals, and a three-room suite of offices. The paid staff consists of the minister, a secretary, and the custodian. Obviously this pastor is chained to the building and cannot find time to do the pastoral calling that he would like to do and that the congregation would like to see him doing. He is busy just "oiling the machinery" that is necessary to keep the program going in a plant of this size. The building determines how this pastor spends his time.

On the same side of the city is a slightly larger congregation, also widely scattered, with a similar plant, except that the sanctuary is perhaps the most impressive of any in the city. The staff includes a full-time director of religious education, an assistant minister, two full-time secretaries, and a custodian. Does the pastor of this church make 1,000-1,500 calls a year? It would appear that the larger staff would free him for the pastoral calling which he enjoys, but here again many in the congregation are unhappy because their pastor rarely if ever calls at their homes.

This minister is first of all an administrator and secondly a widely known preacher. The beauty of the church and the impressive qualities of the Gothic sanctuary attract many visitors each Sunday, and the pastor believes his principal responsibility is to deliver a carefully prepared sermon. Actually he spends far more time on church administration than he does on sermon preparation, and most of the home calls he does make are made in his administrative rather than in his pastoral role. For this minister, too, the building has determined how he will spend much of his time.

This principle is an important one for both clergymen and laymen to comprehend. Not only will knowledge of it help relieve some unnecessary tensions, but understanding of it will help a congregation anticipate what will happen if they move out of their small frame church into the proposed

large brick and glass structure of their dreams. This principle also can be a useful guide to a minister who is considering moving from one parish to another. It will help denominational executives understand the unexpected changes in a
pastor's work habits when he moves from one church to
another. It is a major factor to be considered by denominations who are contemplating the establishment of a new
congregation in an urban-renewal or public-housing area or
in new suburban areas where the primary emphasis usually
is on an extensive pastoral calling program.

5. *The most important single factor in determining the
nature and content of the church program is the size of a
congregation.*

While the building usually is the prime factor in determining how the pastor spends his time, membership size
rather than physical facilities tends to be the most influential
factor in determining what organizations will exist, which
will flourish and which are vulnerable as the membership
declines.

In a definitive study of Methodism Alan Waltz discovered
that the size of the community in which the church is located
is far less significant than the size of the congregation in
determining the content of the church's program. He also
demonstrated that as the size of the church membership
increases or decreases the program expands and contracts in
a predictable and consistent manner.[1] This contrasts with the
widely held view that the "effective church" has a broad program offering, while the limited program is a symptom of
ineffectiveness.

If this is a valid general principle it means that the pastor
or the denominational official should temper his enthusiasm

---

[1] "Aspects of the Program of Local Methodist Churches as Related to
Church Membership Size and to Community Size" (Unpublished Ph.D.
dissertation, Northwestern University, 1961.)

with realism when he exhorts the small congregation to organize a men's club, a young adult group, a committee on worship, or some other organization which may be a natural part of the program in the larger churches but which is an "unnatural" part of the program of the small church. For example, Waltz's study indicated that it is an uphill struggle to maintain a men's club in a Methodist church with less than 300 members.

The Sunday worship service is naturally the most essential single element in a church's program and usually the last to be abandoned. The church school is the second most common item in the church's program. Every church has some form of governing board and almost always a board of Christian education and a finance committee. But small congregations and those which are declining in strength frequently do not have active committees on evangelism, membership, or missions. Survival as a worshiping and as a social institution takes precedence over mission and outreach.

In brief, most local churches should not plan to duplicate the program of a large and "successful" neighbor; rather they should plan realistically for what is needed *and can be achieved* by a church of their size and strength. After all, organization and program are but a means to an end, not the end.

6. *The number of paid staff members in a local church is determined primarily by the financial resources of the membership rather than by need or by the number of members.*

Perhaps one of the most common questions asked of the church planner comes from the young growing congregation which says, "When should we add a second minister to our staff?" In such a question the word "when" refers not to a date on the calendar, but rather to a specific point in the congregation's growth. Should they call a second person when they pass the 800 mark or should they wait until they have 1,200 members?

The phrasing of the question tempts one to offer a rule of thumb ratio, and some persons have suggested that the growth pattern of a congregation will be determined by the number of persons on the staff. This is certainly an attractive answer, and obviously one can work out correlations between the size of staff and the number of members which appear to support this theory—or at least appear to until someone raises the question of which is cause and which is effect. Some experts in the field of church administration also have devised schedules which indicate the ideal ratio of staff to members.

Such answers are all too simple, however, and too pat to satisfy. Experience indicates there are only two generalizations on this matter which are completely valid: (1) Quality is far more important than quantity, and (2) with the exception of a relatively few congregations receiving denominational assistance, the size of the staff of a local church is determined by the ability and willingness of the congregation to pay the cost.

Neither of these two generalizations makes any reference to need; in fact, the almost universal acceptance of the second generalization prevents any consideration of need. If a small congregation with two affluent members is able and willing to pay a salary of 6,000 dollars per year they can be sure of having a full-time pastor. On the other hand, a much larger congregation located in a depressed mining or agricultural area may be able to raise only 2,000 dollars for salary and thus is forced to limp along as part of a circuit or with a part-time supply pastor. Similarly the 700-member church in a wealthy suburb with scores of leaders in the congregation may have two, three, or even four full-time professional staff members and two or three other employees while the inner-city church seeking to minister to hundreds of multi-problem families may be served by one man who is a combination preacher – janitor – educator – parish-caller – counselor – mimeograph-operator – administrator.

Only if and when this self-evident principle is recognized will churchmen be able to deal effectively with a number of problems which plague Protestantism today. The staff-membership ratio is a manifestation of a condition which affects the work of the church in many ways and is a factor in problems which range from reaching the unchurched in the inner city to ministerial status symbols.

The underlying condition is the almost totally unrestrained pattern of congregational autonomy which prevails in Protestantism and says in effect that each church is entitled to as much building and as many staff members as the congregation is willing and able to pay for. (For a more detailed analysis of this point see Chapter 7.)

7. *There is no such thing as an "optimum number of members" which can be applied as a general principle in planning for church growth.*

One of the most common questions addressed to a church planner is, "What is the *right* size for a local church?"

This question can be answered in two ways. An immediate reaction is to offer an opinion, an opinion which obviously reflects personal preferences. Many people prefer churches which have between 350 and 600 members. Such a church is large enough that in most circumstances it can be self-supporting and can carry its financial share of the denomination's total benevolence program, and it is small enough that the members can know one another and that every member can find a place where his talents are needed and each can be confronted with both the challenge for personal spiritual growth and the opportunity for response through service. Such a church is large enough to have a varied educational program which can meet the needs of all age groups; it can justify and finance the erection of a building large enough to house a varied program and yet be small enough that the members can conceive of the building as their "church home." One might go on to cite studies which indicate that smaller congregations have a better record of participation in such areas as the Sunday morning worship and in Christian education. This is not the best answer to this question, however.

This question of the proper size of a church can best be answered by pointing out that the history of Protestantism demonstrates that it can reach all persons only through a many-faceted approach. This has involved large congregations and small congregations, Lutheran churches and Episcopal churches, rural churches and city churches, new churches and old churches, big buildings and no buildings. Such a generalization provides a historical basis for helping one to realize that there is no "right" size and that service not size is the goal of the church. The gospel can and must be preached and the sacraments administered in congregations of all sizes if the word of Christ is to be brought to all men everywhere.

Thus the local church which is concerned about this question would be well advised to forget about attaining and maintaining the "right" size and to concentrate on discovering what special task God has placed before their church in this time and place.

8. *There is only one effective way to limit the size of the membership in a local church.*

Despite the warning expressed earlier some congregations will want to "level off" when they reach a certain membership figure. The usual procedure is to de-emphasize or halt the evangelism efforts of the pastor and congregation as soon as the self-imposed ceiling is reached. All too often this becomes a slow form of suicide, for once a church has given up its sense of evangelism it may very easily lose its sense of mission and purpose. When this occurs it is extremely difficult to avoid the blight of institutionalism.

The observations of church planners and denominational officials indicate that the most effective way to limit membership is to share in the organization of new congregations by "sending out colonization teams." This not only provides the basis for forming a new congregation; it also permits the mother church to continue a vigorous evangelism program without going above its membership ceiling and keeps alive the sense of mission and the awareness that the local church is not an isolated outpost, but is a vital and contributing part of the universal church.

9. *The ratio of local churches to population in an area rarely is less than one church per 1,000 residents.*

Since the end of World War II there has been a great emphasis on organizing new suburban congregations. Literally thousands of new churches have sprung up on the outskirts of the great metropolitan areas of America. In an effort to keep up with the suburban population explosion there have been a number of efforts to devise a simple formula which would enable one to determine how many new churches should be planned for each new community. The most common efforts have used either people or houses as the base for such calculations; i.e. "one new church for each increase of 3,500 in the population" or "one new church for each 1,200 new homes."

While there is no question about the sincerity of those who sought or devised such yardsticks, there is a real question as to the relevance of such rules of thumb. In the United States in 1960, according to figures compiled by the National Council of Churches, there were at least 318,600 local churches. Actually the number is well in excess of that figure, for their compilation does not include all religious bodies, nor does it include the thousands of completely independent local congregations which have no relationship with any other ecclesiastical group. On the basis of a national population of 180,000,000 in 1960 this produces a ratio of one church for every 500 to 600 persons. Studies of small areas indicate that the ratio may range from one church per 400 residents in inner-city neighborhoods of New York, Cleveland, Detroit, and Chicago and in many rural areas, to one church per 2,000 residents in some suburban areas.

This does not mean that one church per 500 to 1,000 residents is a recommended or desirable ratio, but experience does indicate that in most areas this will be the result. If this principle does reflect reality, then perhaps the appropriate question is not, "How many new churches are you recommending to be started in this area?" but rather, "This is how many new churches will be organized in this area if it follows the normal pattern—who is going to accept responsibility for helping them get started?" How much of this responsibility does main-line Protestantism feel it should accept?

10. *The institutional nature of the local church must be recognized in planning for interchurch relationships.*

While some churches show less evidence of institutionalism than others, most local churches do tend to react in certain situations in an institutional manner, and this is of particular interest to anyone working with two or more local churches.

Whether he is the pastor of a two church circuit, a denominational executive, a layman charged with coordinating the activities of two or more local churches, or an employee of an interdenominational agency, today's churchman will find his task easier if he understands that certain reactions of a local church are determined by its institutional nature. A few examples will clarify this.

The natural channels of communications for most agencies and organizations in our society are vertical. This applies to most institutions in our world, and Protestantism is no exception. Thus it should not be surprising to discover that most churchmen have a much more intimate relationship with their denomination and with other congregations and pastors in their denominations than they have with the pastor and members of a nearby church of a different denomination.

This explains why most efforts to develop an interchurch program for a neighborhood run into difficulty if the plan calls for the involvement of churches from several denominations. It also helps one to understand why some denominations prefer to develop an inner-city strategy within the confines of their own communion rather than to share in an interdenominational program. An understanding of this principle of institutional life helps one to see why local churches often are comparatively oblivious to the programs and work of secular institutions working in the same area.

A second example of the normal behavior of an institution is that most organizations which are financially self-supporting tend to be completely autonomous when making decisions. This is the source of one of the major problems of government in metropolitan areas where the number and variety of financially independent units of government make coordination of effort difficult or impossible. This helps to explain why some health and welfare agencies are able to withstand the pressure to make their financial drive a part of the united appeal.

Similarly local churches which are financially self-supporting tend to be highly autonomous and may or may not cooperate with the plans and programs of the denomination. This makes it rather difficult to implement a denominational strategy for a community. Such a comprehensive plan may be prepared with great skill and care, but unless the local churches are closely involved in its preparation it may never be implemented. Regardless of the alleged polity of their denomination, most local churches tend to be congregational in fact. Recently the officials of one denomination which has an episcopal form of church government read in the newspapers of the plans of one of their local churches to relocate. This was the first they had heard of the proposal, but there was nothing they could do about it because the congregation was prepared to finance the move without denominational assistance.

This fact of church life is extremely important to anyone serving in either a denominational or an interdenominational capacity and working with both local churches and denominational agencies.

If one recognizes the combined impact of these two trends —the dominance of vertical channels of communication and the high degree of congregational autonomy of local churches —it is not surprising to discover that many local churches are afflicted with a major problem as a result of their institutional nature. This problem is one of isolation, which often finds each church operating as though it were the only outpost on the frontier. The congregation makes its decisions from the narrow perspective of its own view of the world rather than as a branch of the universal church. This isolation is a contributing factor to the periods of despair and defeat which afflict so many congregations. When a congregation is largely isolated from the rest of the Christian movement, is it any wonder that members doubt that they can convert the world all by themselves?

11. *Local churches, and denominations, tend to become institutionalized, and as this happens they become subject to the effects of institutional blight.*

One of the tragic failures of churchmen today is to recognize that by its nature the local Protestant church is both a part of the body of Christ and a secular organization; the church is both a called-out community in which the Word is preached and the sacraments are duly administered and a highly institutionalized human organization.

Every church member who is involved in helping his local church plan for its future should be aware of this factor of institutionalization and of the blighting effects it may have on the congregation. Without an appreciation of this factor it will be difficult to understand the perspective of many members of the congregation. It may even be impossible to communicate with them.

Institutional blight is an affliction which plagues many organizations, not just churches, and is a growing problem in our society, in which formal organizations play such an important part in the private lives of most individuals. This malady takes many forms, and only a few are peculiar to Protestant churches.

Perhaps the most common form of institutional blight is that the instinct for self-preservation becomes the dominant motive in decision making. In the church this will mean that alternative courses of action are selected, not on the basis of service in the name of Christ, but on the basis of increasing the institutional strength of the church. "What is good for this church is good for Christ" might be the appropriate motto in these circumstances.

This form of institutional blight is rather easily recognized, for the symptoms are obvious. "If our church doesn't begin to reach more of the newcomers in the community it will die." "We can't undertake a building program until we have a larger membership." "We won't be able to meet the new budget unless we get more members." "We can't start a Friday-night youth canteen in our church; those kids would wreck the building!" These are the words one hears in the church which has been afflicted with institutional blight. The perpetuation of the church becomes the paramount concern, and this perspective encourages church members to view people as things to be exploited and manipulated rather than as children of God whom the church should be serving.

Institutional blight may be seen in the deliberations of the local church long-range planning committee as it limits its agenda to discussions of property needs, budget, and membership without ever considering such issues as purpose, mission, and outreach. The means dominate the planning process, and no attention is given to goals.

Another form of the affliction grows out of the recent church building boom which has altered our theology of the church to fit the architect's conception of a good church plant. Nearly everyone has been persuaded that the appropriate form for a church plant is a three unit building which provides space for worship, education, and fellowship. All too frequently after churchmen have been immersed in the mechanics of a building program for a long time they come to think of the church and its purposes as reflections of the building design. Recently a layman was heard defending the need for the church in the world on the basis of its threefold purpose—worship, education, and fellowship. He never once used the words Christ, evangelism, sin, Bible, missions, stewardship, witness, or salvation. His theology had been warped by institutional blight.

The antidote for institutional blight is a rather simple prescription and is widely available. It can be found in the New Testament definition of the church as a community of persons called by God and filled with the Holy Spirit (Acts 20:28; II Cor. 1:1; Acts 2:1). The Christian congregation must remember and act on the biblical premise that it is dependent on the triune God and that each member is dependent upon all other members, past, present, and future. When it forgets this and regards itself as an independent and autonomous organization it becomes highly vulnerable to the ravages of institutional blight.

12. *The geographical parish no longer is the most meaningful basis for describing the people served by a local church in Protestantism.*

Traditionally a local church has drawn its members from a relatively small area, and the congregation could best be described in geographical terms. This is still true of Orthodox Judaism, of most Roman Catholic churches, and of some Protestant churches. It is still the basis on which many new suburban church sites are chosen and by which "comity" decisions are made.

For some time, however, it has been apparent to many outside observers that local churches in Protestantism reflected a definite social-class orientation. There have been a number of sociological studies of communities which revealed that each local church serves a definite social class. More recently other studies have shown the same class bias of several denominations.

While many new congregations start out to serve everyone, or at least all persons who have a preference for that particular denomination, who lives within a mile or two or three of the church, they soon reach the stage where a much more meaningful basis for describing the common characteristics of the membership is a nongeographical measurement. Place of residence usually becomes less important than does social class, nationality or ethnic background, income, theology, sentimental ties, race, or region of birth in determining where the Protestant residents of an area go to church. In one suburban city of 40,000 population it was discovered that over one half of the people attending a particular Protestant church on the typical Sunday morning did not live in the city, and nearly one half of the city residents left the city when they went to church.[2]

While this trend has become obvious to the close observer of Protestantism, it has been largely disregarded in the actual dynamics of church planning. There frequently is validity in the oft proclaimed affirmation that a church should serve the people in its neighborhood; however, there is a real question as to whether a single local church can be expected to serve all the people in an area. This concept of the parish as a geographical entity may be the most misleading principle used by churchmen in their planning. This is not to imply that a congregation should consciously ignore people living near the church, but it may very well suggest that the geographical parish concept takes too much for granted. It may well be that many congregations should ask themselves, "Can we best fulfill God's purpose for our church by concentrating on geographical considerations and ignoring the other divisions which separate men?"

13. *New churches tend to reach the newcomers, and particularly the residents of new housing, while older congregations tend to be made up largely of "old-timers."*

This is another basis for the comment that one cannot accept each church as a fixed unit equal to all other units in church planning. There are exceptions to this statement—sometimes a new congregation ages prematurely; sometimes an old congregation goes through a renewal process and thus is able to reach newcomers. These exceptions tend to be a minority of all churches.

Thus as rural communities become urban with the geographical growth of our metropolitan areas it means that old

[2] For an extremely illuminating and provocative discussion of the place of the geographical parish in American Protestantism see Martin E. Marty, *Second Chance for American Protestantism* (New York: Harper & Row, Publishers, 1963).

congregations in once rural villages will be confronted with the challenge of urbanism. Churchmen should plan either (1) to organize new congregations to minister to the newcomers, or (2) to help the old churches renew themselves so they can do this.

14. *A denomination will achieve a deeper penetration into the total population with many smaller churches than with a few larger congregations.*

Larger churches tend to be more selective in their appeal and tend (there are many exceptions!) to draw lightly from over a large area while small congregations tend to reach more people in a specific area. Furthermore, the larger number of churches provides a larger number and a greater variety of points of contact with the unchurched.

A good illustration of this is to contrast the slow growth of urban Methodism, which tends toward large congregations, and the rapid growth of the Wesleyan and Free Methodist churches and the Church of the Nazarene (all three, like Methodism, developed out of the Wesleyan tradition), which tend toward small congregations.

Thus if growth is the goal churchmen should plan for many small congregations; if a broad and varied program is the goal they should plan for fewer but larger congregations.

These fourteen principles are presented, not as rigid rules, but as generalizations based on experience which may be useful guides to churchmen who are entrusted with the responsibility of planning for the future of Christ's church.

6

Yardsticks in Local Church Planning
+++

"WE HAVE STUDIED A NUMBER OF DIFFERENT PHASES OF THE life of our church, and we believe we are doing pretty well on church attendance. We find that a substantial number of our members live within a mile of the church, and we discovered nearly two thirds of our new members join by letter of transfer. On finances, our average giving per member is nearly eight dollars per year below the national average for our denomination, but our church has had a consistently good record on benevolence giving."

With these comments the chairman of the self-study committee at St. John's concluded his report to the special congregational meeting which had been called to hear and discuss findings of this committee. The members of the self-study team had spent over three months gathering data and drawing maps showing the geographical distribution of members, new members, leaders, and Sunday-school pupils. They had charted membership and attendance patterns for the past decade. They had prepared a half-dozen graphs showing trends in giving patterns, benevolences, and the changing amounts allocated for various budget items.

The result was an impressive and, to some members of the congregation, a confusing array of charts, graphs and maps which appeared to uncover every statistical fact that one could desire about St. John's Church.

However as the discussion continued it became clear that many people were having difficulty understanding the full implications of the data. The questions directed to the self-study committee reflected this.

"You say that our church attendance record is good because each year shows an increase in attendance over the preceding year. Maybe we were so low to start with that we are just now getting up to average. How does our attendance compare with that of other churches?"

"I was interested in your comment that two thirds of our new members come in by transfer. Is this good or bad?"

"How good is our 'good record' on benevolence giving? I have always had the feeling that we should be giving more to missions. What do you think about this?"

"I believe that your comment that our average giving per member is poor because it is below the national average is misleading. We have an awful lot of people on the roll who never come near the church. Don't you think our inflated membership list explains why our per-member average is low?"

Gradually the members of the self-study committee realized that they had completed only one half of their task. They had carefully measured many different characteristics of the congregation at St. John's, but they had failed to provide the congregation with adequate performance standards against which their church could be evaluated. They needed some kind of yardstick which would help them measure what was happening at St. John's.

Actually their plight was not as bad as it appeared, for they did possess two sets of useful yardsticks for their self-appraisal. First they had an *internal* set of comparisons. The committee had gathered material covering several different years, and thus it was possible to compare the current year's record with that of previous years in several areas. For example, the church attendance records showed an actual increase in the number of persons attending Sunday morning services for each of the past six years. Furthermore, this was not entirely due to an increase in membership because the ratio of attendance to membership had climbed from 37 per cent to 43 per cent during this period.

Second, many members felt that they should be guided by *absolute* standards. Several of the members judged the attendance pattern and other presentations on this basis. They contended that the biblical requirement for each member to be in church each Sunday was quite clear, and therefore, the church attendance figure should be as large as the membership figure, perhaps larger since many persons who were not counted as confirmed members usually were present for Sunday worship. They also pointed out that the giving level represented at most less than one fifth of a tithe of the aggregate congregational income.

Throughout the discussion, however, there continued to be requests that the information be interpreted in terms of what other churches were doing. They were seeking a third type of standards. These members wanted a *comparative* set of measurements so they could view what was happening at St. John's in terms of what was happening in other Protestant churches. These yardsticks can be developed, but they should be used with some degree of caution. *They do represent what churches in America are doing; they do not repre-*

sent what the churches should be doing. They describe what is rather common, not what is ideal!

The evangelical mission of the church is a primary concern in Christianity, and therefore, this merits first consideration. Three useful yardsticks are baptisms, source of new members, and number of persons received on profession of faith. (Here comparisons must be limited to Protestant denominations which approve the baptism of infants and which receive young people into full membership at about age twelve or thirteen.)

National averages reveal that the typical Lutheran, Presbyterian, or Methodist church will average about forty baptisms per year for each 1,000 members. Thus a 300-member congregation such as St. John's should expect to average about twelve baptisms per year, perhaps fourteen or fifteen since smaller congregations tend to register a higher ratio of baptisms than do larger congregations. The spread among denominational groups is not as great as some might expect. The American Lutheran Church reports about fifty baptisms per 1,000 confirmed members compared to forty per 1,000 for the Lutheran Church in America and the Evangelical United Brethren Church, to thirty-six per 1,000 for the United Presbyterians and Methodists, and to fifty baptisms per 1,000 *communicant* members for the Episcopal Church.

The people at St. John's had been told that two thirds of their new members had joined by transfer. An analysis of denominational and individual local church records reveals that this is a high ratio. Perhaps the people at St. John's were spending too much time trying to build up the membership total and too little time trying to reach the unchurched. Usually a self-study will reveal that a majority of the new members joined by confession of faith (or were restored to the roll) and somewhat less than 50 per cent came in by

letter of transfer. The two major exceptions to this Protestant pattern are in Methodist churches, where a slight
majority of the new members usually are transfers, and in
suburban communities, where transfers sometimes outnum-
ber those joining by confession of faith by as much as a two
to one margin.

St. John's thought of itself as a church which was quite
effective in reaching the people who lived near the church;
however, a good many members had moved away to newer
and better homes. Most of them now lived beyond three
miles from the church, but continued to be faithful members. How can the church measure its effectiveness in reaching the people in the neighborhood?

The best answer to this question would require a survey
of the neighborhood to discover how many unchurched persons live near St. John's. There are, however, two yardsticks
available which will provide a good indication of whether
or not St. John's is really a neighborhood-oriented ministry.
The first is to locate on a map the homes of each church
attender. Do at least one half of the attenders live within a
mile of the church? They should if St. John's is really a
neighborhood church. Is there any difference in the residence
pattern of the regular attenders and of those who attend less
than one fourth of the time? If the majority of the regular
attenders live beyond a mile, it indicates that St. John's probably is moving away from its old role as a neighborhood
church.

A far better yardstick is to examine the place of residence
and the tenure of the leaders. If more than one half of the
leaders live outside the neighborhood it may mean that the
church is either seeking the best available leadership or ignoring the potential problems caused by unlimited tenure
rather than taking the trouble to recruit and develop indigenous local leadership. If more than one third of the

leaders have been holding the same office for over three years perhaps insufficient attention is being given to the opportunities the church offers people to grow in a knowledge and understanding of Christ and his church through responsible service in the church.

Perhaps the most useful yardstick in evangelism is the number of persons who join on confession of faith or who are restored to the roll after having been removed. (This combines the new converts and the reconverted backsliders.) Two Lutheran groups—the Lutheran Church in America and the American Lutheran Church—average between fifty and fifty-five such new members per 1,000 members compared to forty-four for the United Presbyterians, forty for the Evangelical United Brethren and thirty-five for the Methodists. While local churches do vary from these averages, the size of the congregation or the degree of urbanization appears to be much less important than the evangelical spirit of the members and the pastor. (Here again varying degrees of strictness in defining "members" affects the averages. This accounts for part of the gap between the Lutherans and the Methodists.)

The usual method of comparing church attendance figures across congregational boundaries is to translate the average number of persons attending the Sunday morning worship services into a percentage of the total confirmed membership. Thus at St. John's the current average attendance of 129 was equal to 43 per cent of the confirmed membership of 300. Is this high or low, good or bad?

The answer to these questions varies from denomination to denomination. Worship attendance at Lutheran churches tends to average around 55 per cent of the total membership compared to about 45 to 50 per cent for United Presbyterian churches and 40 per cent for the Methodists. There are many variations within each denominational family, however.

Rural churches often have higher attendance-to-membership ratios than city churches. New churches usually do better than old churches, and it is not at all unusual for a new congregation of 100 to 300 members to have an average attendance percentage ranging from 60 per cent to 80 per cent. Small congregations frequently boast of a higher church attendance percentage than do large congregations, and Negro congregations often have a much higher attendance ratio than white congregations. Poor churches tend to do better than wealthy congregations.

These wide variations do limit the usefulness of church attendance in comparing one congregation with another; however, church attendance averages and percentages often are helpful in historical comparisons of the same congregation. Average church attendance—that is, the average number of persons present for the Sunday morning worship service—is almost always a much more meaningful figure than membership and, therefore, is a useful base figure in developing other yardsticks, especially on stewardship and finances.

It is more difficult to generalize on stewardship patterns because varying economic circumstances are reflected in the dollar level of giving. When the sample is restricted to urban and suburban congregations in which most members have a family income of 4,000 to 10,000 dollars per year, a remarkably consistent three-part pattern begins to emerge, however, *especially if average attendance rather than membership is used as a base.*

1. The actual receipts of a majority of such churches average between 150 and 200 dollars times the average attendance at worship on Sunday morning. Thus a congregation with an average church attendance of 200 usually will have total annual receipts ranging between 30,000 and 40,000 dollars.

2. Congregations which fall below the 150-dollar level often report that their biggest problem is one of finances, and an examination of the church program almost invariably reveals inadequacies because of the lack of program funds.

3. Many congregations do top the 200-dollar level, and an examination of their recent history frequently reveals either (1) that a systematic stewardship campaign was carried on by a broadly based group within the congregation during the past few years (perhaps with the increased receipts to go to a building program or some other special fund) or (2) that an effective effort has been made to deepen the spiritual life of the members, perhaps through use of the small Bible-study and prayer groups.

The two major exceptions to this pattern are (1) some small rural and inner-city congregations where the giving level averages around 100 dollars or less per average attender, and (2) large city churches with an active building program which frequently top the 250 dollars per average attender level.

Generalizations on total giving can be made without reference to denominational labels; however, yardsticks on benevolence giving must be developed within a denominational framework because of distinctions in defining what constitutes a benevolence gift. For example, in some denominations the local church's contribution toward the salaries of denominational officials or toward the pensions of retired ministers is counted as benevolence giving; in other denominations it is not.

Local churches in Protestantism "send away" about one fifth to one sixth of their total receipts to support various missionary, denominational, and interdenominational activities. Currently there is considerable support by many congregations to raise their contributions to "outside" causes to one dollar for each one dollar spent locally. Others are committed to equally dividing all nonbuilding receipts, while a third group has adopted the "one for two" plan of designating one dollar for benevolences for every two dollars the congregation spends on itself. There are also many congregations which contribute as little as one tenth or less of their total receipts to benevolent causes.

Another helpful yardstick in measuring benevolence giving is to calculate the annual contribution per member. Precautions must be taken, however, in making comparisons across denominational lines. For example, the per-member average for benevolence giving in the United Presbyterian Church, U.S.A., is about eighteen dollars per confirmed member, slightly higher than the average for the Lutheran Church in America. But the difference is larger than it first appears because of the stricter definition of membership used by most Lutheran churches. Northern urban churches frequently reach the fifteen to twenty-five dollars per member range in benevolence giving, but many congregations fail to reach even the fifteen-dollar level except in rare years. For the nation as a whole the average is about twelve to fifteen dollars per member.

More useful for comparison purposes than the per-member average is the annual contribution to benevolences per average attender. This method avoids the variance growing out of widely differing standards used in defining membership. Local churches in Protestantism tend to contribute between thirty and fifty dollars *per average attender* for benevolences and for denominational and interdenominational activities. This is a rather wide range, but the differences among denominations are rather striking. The Lutherans, the Presbyterians, and some independent congregations tend to give much more generously to benevolences than do the Congregationalists, the Methodists, and the Disciples of Christ.

While the amount spent by local churches for music varies greatly from congregation to congregation, those with an excellent music program often find themselves spending about 10 per cent of their total local expense budget (exclusive of building fund and benevolences) for music. This is in contrast to the expenditures of the vast majority of local churches which devote less than 2 per cent of their budget to the ministry of music.

Performance standards such as these are intended for the use of the congregation which is examining itself, for the congregation which is seeking to measure and interpret its own strengths and weaknesses. They are intended only to serve as guidelines for the congregation which is developing plans for a more effective program of service. They should not be mistaken as benchmarks of respectability. The obligation of the Christian church is not to be respectable, but to be an effective and evangelical witness for Jesus Christ. Hopefully readers will find these yardsticks helpful as they measure the performance of their own church as it seeks to fulfill this mission.

7

The Dilemma of the Church in the Inner City
+++

DURING THE EARLY 1950's THE PROBLEM OF THE CHURCH IN the inner city was regarded as a phenomenon of the Northeastern part of the United States. Most of the local churches that were breaking new trails in the inner city were located in such places as New York, Chicago, New Haven, Cleveland, Detroit, Boston, Milwaukee, and Toledo. To a substantial extent these cities are still the scene of a large share of the creative efforts to develop new methods for ministering to the residents of the inner city. The blight which appears to be an inseparable element of the inner city is spreading out to other parts of the nation, however, and suddenly churchmen in Atlanta, Louisville, Denver, Omaha, Oklahoma City, Dallas, and other cities have discovered that they too are faced with the dilemma of planning for the church in the inner city.

The emergence of the inner city as a unique situation calling for specialized attention from the church is the result of a variety of factors and forces. The exodus of stable, home-owning middle-class families to the suburbs usually is cited as the prime cause. There are many other significant forces, however—some of these were discussed in Chapter 2. Other factors such as the shortened workweek, the pressures of contemporary advertising, the decline of the public educational system in many central cities, the lack of resident leadership, the increase in chronic unemployment among unskilled and semiskilled workers, discrimination in housing and employment, and the lack of adequate enforcement of housing and building codes have contributed to the inner-city problem. While an awareness of the causes of current and past problems is essential to effective planning, attention must first be directed to the many-faceted dilemma in which Protestants find themselves as they attempt to plan for the future of the church in the inner city.

Church leaders caught in this dilemma ask a variety of complex questions. Is the inner city already overchurched? Is there really a need for new churches in the inner city? Where will the money come from to support an enlarged ministry in the inner city? Is it reasonable to expect churches in the inner city to be self-supporting? Is the storefront an answer to the problems of capital costs and accessibility? Are the problems confronting the inner-city pastor really different from those facing his colleague in other parts of urban America? Answers to all these questions are complicated by the blight which characterizes the inner city.

While urban renewal and public housing have resulted in some drastic alterations in the urban landscape, there are still vast areas of blight which have been untouched by the various proposals for rebuilding urban America. For example, planners report that 15 per cent of the land area of

Detroit is blighted; in Cleveland the comparable figure is 18 per cent. Similar figures are reported by planners in other cities, but only a small fraction of this blighted area is undergoing urban renewal treatment.

In all too many of these slum neighborhoods main-line Protestantism has already fled. Evidence of its former presence and past glories can be seen in the large masonry buildings which remain. Some have been sold to Negro congregations or to sect groups; some have been converted to warehouses, funeral homes, and offices; and a few stand abandoned with "For Sale" signs prominently displayed.

Not all the congregations have completely abandoned the inner city, but many of those remaining serve a constituency drawn largely from outside their neighborhood. Unless these congregations are able and willing to undertake a neighborhood-oriented ministry they have little relevance to the process by which Protestantism plans for its future in the inner city.

The Staff Question

Perhaps the first consideration which must be discussed in planning for the church in the inner city is the issue of "overchurching." It is easy for an observer to make a windshield survey of the inner city and come away feeling, "The buildings may not be the best, but there certainly are enough churches there." This is superficially true. In most slum neighborhoods there is one congregation for every 400 to 500 residents—in contrast with the suburban average of one church per 1,000 residents. This is a deceptive figure. A better index is the ratio of full-time, trained, professional staff persons per thousand residents. In suburbia there usually will be one such person for every 700 residents; in the inner city one for every 2,000 to 3,000 residents.

The inner city, like rural America, is overchurched and

understaffed. It is not at all unusual to find sixty congregations, half of them meeting in storefronts, theaters, or residences, in an inner-city neighborhood with a population of 25,000. Perhaps a score of these churches will have the services of a full-time pastor, and only five or six will have more than one full-time, professional staff person. Several of the churches with a full-time minister will be ministering to a nonresident congregation, and thus the number of full-time ministers serving the residents is even smaller than it appears.

It becomes apparent that the primary issue in planning for the future of Protestantism in these blighted inner-city areas centers around the question of staff. What is the appropriate ratio of staff to population? What is the role of a staff person in an inner-city church?

Both questions are extremely difficult and cannot be answered separately, for the number of staff persons needed will depend on their roles. If one considers only the articulated *wants* of the residents preaching and home visitation are the principal duties that are expected of the inner-city pastor. On this basis one clergyman per 1,200 to 1,500 residents would appear to be an appropriate ratio. This is only one half the typical suburban ratio where the *demands* of the congregation force many churches to move to a multiple staff.

If one considers, however, not the expressed *wants* of the inner-city residents, but rather their real *needs,* a ratio of one full-time professional staff person per 300 residents may be required to carry on an adequate ministry. In addition to preaching, calling, and general church administration there are many unexpressed needs. In the typical suburban community there is usually a plethora of leadership for community affairs, for initiating and executing program ideas in the local church, and for carrying out responsibilities.

By contrast in the inner city there is usually a deficit of leadership, and a valid ministry will be concerned with recruiting and training indigenous leadership, with helping to create and maintain a structure of community organization, and with initiating and implementing relevant church program proposals. In addition, the concentration of dependent, multi-problem families means that the ministry of pastoral care will be both time consuming and emotionally exhausting.

The Dilemma of the Inner-City Pastor

Far more crucial than finances or building facilities is the matter of pastoral leadership. All too often a man will be called or appointed to serve an inner-city congregation without anyone's having considered the dilemma in which the new minister may find himself. "Telling the story is romantic, but living the life is hell," remarked one of the most effective inner-city pastors in the Lutheran Church in America.

What are the conditions which make the task of the inner-city pastor so difficult? Typically he finds himself working with a congregation most of whom have moved away from the neighborhood of the church and some of whom never lived in that neighborhood. Not infrequently the original congregation was composed largely of one nationality group, and this identification is still obvious in the present congregation. In many instances the church building is old, expensive to maintain, and not suited to present-day needs. The members—and also the pastor—usually come from a social and economic strata that is quite different from that of the people living near the church.

In this situation the minister is expected to be the pastor of a successful and effective church. Many churchmen define a successful church as one that is self-supporting, is making a decent contribution to the denomination's missionary and promotional program, and is growing in numbers. A common current definition of an effective church is one that ministers to the people in the neighborhood of the church.

If the pastor is to have a church that is financially self-supporting he apparently must depend on the resources of the nonresident members. He is further dependent on this group for leadership in the governing board, administration, church school, and the other organizations of the church. If the pastor neglects these nonresident members he is likely to lose them to a church nearer their homes. If he spends the required time with this segment of his membership he has very few hours left for the time-consuming door-to-door calling necessary to reach the changing population in the neighborhood of his church. He may suggest to the nonresident member the opportunity to serve Christ by giving his time, talent, and money to his old church that is now a mission outpost in the heart of the city. At the same time, however, a denominational official may be offering this same member a challenge to serve the same Christ by helping to organize a new suburban congregation. The member may also hear another church leader suggest that all good churchmen attend the church nearest their homes. In this situation should the pastor spend his time on the people who provide the leadership and financial resources for his church or on the people in his neighborhood?

Even if the pastor is able to retain the loyalty of his nonresident members and still have time for calling in the neighborhood he is faced with other questions. Should the program of the church be tailored to the people in the neighborhood or to the old members? Should he use hymns or gospel songs in the worship service? What kind of literature should he use in the church school? Should he agree to have separate organizations—youth, women, men, choir—for the old members apart from those organized for the newcomers to the neighborhood? Or should he practice what he preaches about the fellowship of Christians?

The minister's role is further complicated by the differences between his view of the church and that held by many of his people. Under the best of circumstances it is difficult to put into practice the concept of a classless church ministering to all the needs of every person. It is even more difficult in an urban society that has rigid class lines and tends to separate the "spiritual" from the everyday aspects of life.

Another facet of the dilemma is the image of the pastor. In many instances it appears that the congregation wants the minister to fulfill a priestly role, whereas the pastor feels constrained to stand also in the prophetic tradition. The former stands for things as they are or used to be; the latter proclaims what God wants them to be. Is the church to be what its members want it to be or what Paul said it should be? Should the church continue as a link with the past—a church in which Sunday is as much a day of homecoming as it is a day of worship—or should it seek to serve the people in a changing neighborhood?

Finally, the dilemma is compounded by the pastor's relations with his denomination and his neighboring ministers. If he seeks financial aid from the denomination for his church he must usually prove himself to be an acceptable risk. This may involve two or three years of extensive service on various boards, committees, and commissions through which he gains the recognition necessary for the approval of his request. Moreover, the pastor may be very ecumenically minded. What should be his relationship with the fundamentalist churches in his community? The suburban minister can ignore them, but the inner-city pastor often finds that many of these churches were organized to serve the same newcomers he is trying to reach. Can he better under-

stand the needs of these new residents by associating with
ministers from these independent fundamentalist churches?
Or should he limit his professional relationships to ministers
of other main-line denominations? Or should he devote this
portion of his schedule to activities within his denomination,
since it is likely that any chance for real assistance is almost
certainly limited to denominational channels?

These are some of the questions and conditions which
make the task of the inner-city pastor both complex and
contradictory. They create a dilemma which is very real
and which must be understood by anyone seeking to help
plan for Protestantism in the inner city. Only if one compre-
hends the variety and intensity of the pressures on the inner-
city pastor can he begin to plan intelligently for the future
of the church there.

These difficult choices which confront the inner-city pastor
are paralleled by the questions facing many churchmen at
both the congregational and the denominational levels of
Protestantism. Any consideration of the many facets of the
problems facing Protestantism in the inner city reveals an
increasingly complex condition, but a situation which calls
for positive planning and inspired action *now*. The people
are there; they need the gospel; and the church has no alternative but to respond. Some of the conditions may be altered
with the passage of time, but this is no excuse for delay in
responding to the challenge of the inner city.

The planning necessary for this response must be based on
a highly knowledgeable comprehension of such secular forces
as blight, urban renewal, public housing and expressways; on
a realistic awareness of the challenge and alternatives confronting the local church as an institution and as a congregation; on a sympathetic understanding of the plight of the
dedicated pastor and the committed laymen who are seeking
to respond to the imperative to minister to the neighbor-

hood; and on an unreserved trust in the power of the Holy Spirit.

Should Every Local Church Be Self-Supporting?

It is obvious that very, very few inner-city congregations will be able to raise the money to pay for the needed staff members. This raises the question of denominational subsidies and leads into a much larger question, Should every local church be self-supporting?

The answers to this are varied. Some churchmen contend that there simply are not sufficient funds available to finance more than a few "pilot projects," and therefore, most new congregations, inner city or suburban, must become self-supporting. Others contend that a perpetual subsidy is detrimental to the spiritual and moral fiber of a congregation, and therefore, for their own good as well as for financial reasons, each congregation must become financially self-supporting. Still others insist that the renewing power of the gospel is strong enough to enable converts to Christ to throw off the shackles of despair, poverty, and slovenly habits. A fourth group takes a more pragmatic view and contends that since each denomination has only limited resources the available funds should be directed to where they will do the most good. Thus results rather than needs will determine how and where mission funds are to be expended. A potential new congregation which promises to grow by fifty or a hundred new members per year and which is likely to become self-supporting before long will have a higher priority than the proposal to begin a new ministry in a slum where half of the families are on relief, where experience indicates that the rate of membership growth is very slow, and where there is little likelihood that the congregation will ever be able to get along without financial assistance.

An increasing number of leaders in Protestantism are recognizing, however, that the same standards and patterns which have worked in new church development in suburbia may not work in the inner city. This is becoming apparent in a variety of ways—in the type of demands made on the pastor's time, the design of the building required to meet the needs of the congregation, the response to door-to-door calling, and the ability of the laity to assume certain responsibilities in initiating, organizing, and carrying out program ideas, but perhaps most of all in terms of church finances. One suggested approach to this problem of church finances is based on the premise that each church does not have to be self-supporting and that it is both necessary and legitimate for some inner-city churches to be financially dependent on their sister churches, perhaps for an indefinite number of years. To some churchmen such a suggestion is heresy, to others it is socialism, but to some it is New Testament Christianity.

This raises both practical and philosophical or theological questions. The practical ones are directed primarily toward enlarging the basis of financing home-mission activities and the basis for dividing the limited resources among several needy efforts.

In the long run, however, the philosophical and theological questions are more important because the answers to these will determine both short-range decisions and long-term policies as the main-line Protestant denominations seek to carry out the great commission.

While there is no question that it would simplify the administrative problems of the denomination if every local church were financially self-supporting, there are some very serious considerations which must be evaluated before one can give unreserved affirmative support to this concept.

First, why should the local church be the unit on which

self-support is measured? Granted this is convenient, but is it consistent with the belief that every Christian is a member of the universal church, not simply a local church? Why not urge that each member be "self-supporting" in terms of his personal contribution to the local church or that the church school, the youth fellowship, and every other organization in the church be self-supporting? (Unfortunately this is the position taken by many laymen and clergymen who apply "businesslike" methods to local church administration!) Better yet, why not use a more inclusive administrative unit such as the synod, the district, the presbytery, or the conference? Such a standard certainly would give the members of the several local churches within that geographical area a better opportunity to know the thrill of *sharing* in the work of the larger church. In fact, of course, this is the actual position adhered to by several denominations in many of their administrative practices. If denominational leaders could discard the stereotype that every local church must become self-supporting and accept the larger jurisdictional unit as the basic unit for financial planning it might decrease their worries and increase the outreach of their denomination.

Perhaps the best parallel is public education. Rarely does an individual local school pay its way. It depends not only on the taxes of the residents of the neighborhood and on the taxes from the commercial and industrial property located in other parts of the district, but also on a certain amount of state aid. The district as a whole must collect enough revenue to pay the bills, but the location, size, staff, and facilities of the individual schools are determined primarily by the needs of the children in the neighborhood rather than by the financial resources of the parents.

A second and much more important consideration concerns the church's mission to those parts of urban America in which are concentrated large numbers of persons with very low incomes. As mentioned earlier some of these people live in low-income public housing. Most of them live in neighborhoods once occupied by middle- and upper-income families who have long since moved to greener pastures taking their churches with them. A large percentage of the current residents of the inner city are eking out a living on substandard income. Often their total income is less than that required to support a family at the minimum level of subsistence which is acceptable in our society. In all America there are between 35 and 38,000,000 citizens in this category. To ask them to support their own churches may literally mean taking the bread out of a child's mouth, the shoes off a baby's feet, or the school supplies out of a boy's hand. Is this necessary when other congregations have 40,000-dollar organs, foam rubber pew cushions, air-conditioned buildings, and stainless steel kitchens? Is it necessary? Is it Christian?

Many of the residents in these ghettoes of poverty depend upon some form of public assistance for all or most of their incomes. Does the church have the right to expect a tithe out of a relief check? Which is the more important principle, congregational self-support or separation of church and state?

The third aspect of this question is often overlooked but is extremely serious. Today as perhaps never before in American church history there is a strong emphasis on the desirability of each local church's ministering to the people in the neighborhood. Couple with this goal the fact that in our urbanized society the poor are concentrated in certain neighborhoods while the well-to-do citizens live elsewhere and it becomes apparent that some churches will have access to far greater financial resources than will others. Therefore, acceptance of the idea that each congregation should be self-supporting can be based only on the assumption that there will be different levels of expenditures and services in churches, or to put it more bluntly, a congregation is entitled to what it can pay for. This suggests that a 500-member congregation which is able and willing to pay for four or five full-time staff persons and a luxurious million-dollar plant is entitled to that level of service while another 500-member congregation drawn from a low-income neighborhood must struggle along with a part-time minister in a secondhand building. Is this in harmony with the New Testament concept of the church?

Finally, this concept of self-support must be examined in light of the patterns of proportionate giving in American Protestantism. The two most common patterns are percentage (the tithe is an example) and per capita askings. While some local church finance committees divide the total anticipated expenditures by the number of members and use the result as the basic goal in the every member canvass, many more congregations ask each person to contribute a percentage of his income to the church. Historically, of course, this has been 10 per cent, but a more common contemporary asking is between 2 and 5 per cent. For benevolences the denomination usually asks either a per capita amount—i.e., six dollars per member—or a percentage of the local church budget. If most of the members of the denomination come from the same economic class it would be hard to criticize either plan.

If, however, a denomination is serious about reaching people in all economic levels in a society in which the wealthiest one tenth of the population shares 27 per cent of the total personal income and the poorest three tenths divide up only 9 per cent, a new and less regressive system of giving must be devised. The progressive income tax of the federal government might serve as a stimulant to rethinking the basis used by denominations in the establishment of benevolence askings for local churches.

Here, too, one can point to many local churches which do contribute to benevolent causes, not on the basis of membership, but rather on the basis of their financial resources. They are to be commended, and may their ranks increase! If more churches join them it may be possible to advance to a more revolutionary method.

While to some this next proposal may sound more socialistic than biblical, a reading of the first five chapters of Acts suggests that perhaps all the Christian churches of one community (of the conference or synod? of the nation? or of the world?) should pool their offerings and use the proceeds for the needs of all of the churches. This would eliminate the distinction between "benevolences" and "local expenses" and the double envelope—but perhaps the double envelope has fostered a double standard?

If the church sought financial support for its ministry on the basis of the individual Christian's ability to contribute to the total work of the universal church, and if it pooled these contributions, it might then be free to carry on a universal ministry to all men everywhere regardless of the economic compartment of society which they occupied. Such a ministry obviously would vary from place to place but its characteristics would be determined more by needs and less by wants—the reverse of which too often is the case today.

Adoption of this proposal might disrupt many a building campaign and upset the bookkeeping systems of most local churches, but it would provide an effective answer to the question, "Should every local church be self-supporting?"

Whether they adopt this proposal or not each denomination must work out an answer to this fundamental question before it can develop a consistent and coherent plan for a continuing ministry in the inner city.

Is the Storefront a Valid Tool?

Closely related to these questions of staff and finances is the matter of a building in which the inner-city congregation will be housed. This is a particularly important question for a denomination planning to re-enter the inner city with a completely fresh start. Some people contend that a conventional building is necessary as a symbol as well as for program activities.

Others have suggested that perhaps any building is a handicap, and that the minister should work out of his apartment, spending his time with people on the streets and in their homes—at least until he sees what kind of program and, therefore, what kind of building would be most appropriate for the needs of his new congregation.

A compromise solution has been offered by a number of churchmen who have suggested the use of storefronts. At first this appeared to be a rather novel approach and was rejected by some tradition-bound persons who felt that the church had to look like a church and avoid any resemblance to a here-today-gone-tomorrow holiness sect.

Here and there a few venturesome persons became convinced of the value of the storefront approach, and it has now been tried out in a number and variety of situations. For example, in the brand-new community of Cape Coral, Florida, a new United Lutheran congregation is housed in a shopping-center storefront, and in Cleveland a storefront serves as "the outpost" for a suburban Methodist church which is seeking to build a closer relationship between the residents of the central city and suburbanites.

Much more common is the storefront in a blighted area of the old central city. On Chicago's near South Side, across the street from a huge slum that recently was cleared and redeveloped with high-rise apartments, stands Christ the

Mediator—in a storefront. This seven-year-old racially integrated United Lutheran congregation owns the old commercial building and plans to raze it and erect a new church to serve some of the 5,000 families who will be living within walking distance of their site. But, the first several years of the new congregation's life are being spent in a storefront.

Perhaps more typical is the Church of Saint Philip the Evangelist in Cleveland. Located between a public-housing development of 1,208 apartments on one side and the city's worst slum on the other, this congregation of the Inner City Protestant Parish (supported by ten Protestant denominations) rents two storefronts, one for worship and Christian education and one for fellowship, youth work, and offices. Much of this church's program—counseling, Bible study, youth work—is carried on in the homes of nearby residents, on the street, and in vacant lots, but the storefronts provide the necessary meeting space for certain other group activities such as worship and Christian education.

How has this idea of using storefronts worked out? Is it a good idea? What are the reactions of the pastors? Enough "experiments" with storefronts have been attempted and sufficient time has elapsed to make possible an appraisal of the storefront approach.

The users have discovered that the storefront has many advantages. These include (1) low cost—no major capital investment, modest operating costs; (2) flexibility—can be used in different ways; (3) mobility—the church can move as environmental conditions change or as demands shift; (4) accessibility—the storefront can be easily reached by people coming to church; (5) familiarity—the storefront is a familiar building; (6) intimacy—newcomers are encouraged to mix, and it enhances a sense of community; (7) program-centered operation—by nature the storefront can be only one of many tools, and the danger of a building-centered program is eliminated.

On the other hand, experience has demonstrated that a storefront operation has many built-in liabilities: (1) image —many persons have had unpleasant experiences with the traditional type of storefront religion, and they automatically reject every new storefront that comes along; (2) youth work —it is almost impossible to carry on an adequate program for children and young people unless adequate physical facilities are available, and the storefront seldom affords such facilities; (3) growth—while the storefront offers certain advantages in terms of intimacy and costs, a concomitant liability has been the limitation on growth in numbers, in variety of program, and in size of program; (4) worship—it is difficult to achieve a suitable atmosphere for Sunday morning worship services if the same facilities have been used for a social gathering on Saturday evening; (5) symbolism— residents of a blighted area need a gathering place that is pleasant and comfortable, and one that allows them to forget their own crowded, squalid quarters. The storefront cannot offer this. Furthermore, many of these persons need an outlet for their creative talents which they do not have in their rented quarters but which they might have in a permanent church plant.

Saint Paul's Community Church, an inner-city congregation in Cleveland, found these limitations to be so serious that they more than offset the advantages inherent in a storefront. This Congregational congregation was organized in 1955 through the efforts of the Inner City Protestant Parish. After the old church which served as their first meeting place was condemned they moved into a storefront a few blocks away. While this facility provided some advantages in reaching nearby residents, the disadvantages prompted the decision to plan a new structure at the old site. The resulting

225,000-dollar structure was made possible through the joint efforts of the congregation, the Cleveland Union of Congregational Churches, and the friends and other denominations supporting the Inner City Protestant Parish. This new building is an outstanding architectural example of how the accessibility and intimacy of the storefront can be combined with the qualities inherent in a new special-purpose structure to provide a church especially suited to the demands of a ministry in the inner city.

One of the most common questions asked about storefronts is, What is the reaction of members of the congregation? Unquestionably the most important single factor in answering this question concerns the permanency of the arrangement. If it is clearly understood by all that the storefront is a temporary arrangement and that eventually a conventional church plant will be purchased or constructed, then the storefront is not a liability. It is true that some people will stay away because of the unconventional image or the inadequate facilities, but their number usually is offset by those who see in this the opportunity for an exciting Christian venture and who are attracted by the challenge. Still others who might not be reached from a conventional building are attracted by the accessibility of the storefront.

On the other hand, if it appears that the storefront will be the permanent meeting place of the congregation there is the possibility that an air of defeatism will prevail and discourage some prospective new members from joining. There is the possibility that some members will see the storefront as a symbol of their own poverty and seek to reject it as soon as it is economically possible for them to do so. Finally, there is the problem of class feeling. "Why does our denomination subsidize the building of new churches for newly organized congregations in suburbia and expect us to put up with this old building?"

It has become obvious that both storefronts and the more conventional church buildings have disadvantages as well as advantages. The decision as to which is better depends on the need.

Thus far the primary need has been to regain a foothold in the inner city. The storefront has provided this opportunity for a number of new congregations. Perhaps equally significant is the recognition that the program should determine the nature of the physical plant rather than, as is too often the case, letting the building determine the church program. As one storefront minister put it, "The kind or type of building doesn't matter; the important thing is for the minister to get out of the building and into the streets."

In general it appears that the storefront has an important and legitimate role in Protestantism's re-entry into the inner city. Experience has demonstrated rather conclusively that most congregations eventually will want to move out of the storefront and into a more appropriate building. The storefront provides the necessary modest beginning point, however; it helps the congregation decide what kind of building they will need; and it encourages strangers to feel the church is truly in their midst. Where the storefront serves these purposes it must be proclaimed a successful and effective tool in the church's mission to the city.

8

*Urban Renewal and the Problem
of Perspective*
+++

"IF WE SHIFT THE SITE FOR THE NEW ELEMENTARY SCHOOL TO
the northwest corner it would be possible for St. Mark's
Church to be left untouched. Of course if they want to stay,
they would have to bring their building up to meet the spec-
ifications of the building code. However, we could provide
for them the opportunity to acquire 40,000 square feet of
land on the east side of their building. If we designate the
alternative reuse purpose to be residential, they should be
able to buy it for thirty-five cents per square foot."

With these words the chief urban renewal planner began
his effort to persuade the city's planning director that the
proposed renewal plan for the near north side should permit
St. Mark's to remain. The church, a sixty-year-old Protestant
congregation, had the only good building of the four

churches within the renewal area. The others were definitely scheduled for demolition.

"The success of our redevelopment plan depends at least in part on the emergence of a sense of community among the residents. That's why we are proposing that a new elementary school be constructed in the area," continued the planner. "The people at St. Mark's can remodel their building and bring it up to code for less than 15,000 dollars. The additional land would enable them to do some landscaping, perhaps to develop a small playground for kids in the area, and to provide some off-street parking. There will be 4,500 people living in this area when it is redeveloped, and there should be at least one church there. St. Mark's is the only real possibility, and I believe we should do all we can to encourage them to stay."

The planner won his point and the final reuse plan not only permitted St. Mark's to remain, but also gave them the opportunity to buy nearly an acre of land for only 14,000 dollars. What was the reaction at St. Mark's?

"Your pastor and I have had at least a dozen meetings with the officials at city hall," said the chairman of the trustees to the members of the official board at St. Mark's, "and we are pleased to report that our church stands to benefit tremendously from the urban renewal program planned for this neighborhood. We will have to raise about 40,000 to 50,000 dollars to carry out our end of the bargain, but I think we can swing that. The trustees have prepared a four-part plan which we are submitting for your consideration. It includes a 12,000-dollar remodeling job for the present building, the purchase from the city of a large parcel of land next door to the church, blacktopping that land to provide 150 spaces of off-street parking, and erecting a steel fence to enclose all our property, including the parking lot. The land will cost

14,000 dollars and the entire program should not cost more than 45,000 dollars if we do part of the work ourselves."

"Why do you want to fence the lot?" asked one member of the board.

"We expect an increase in vandalism here with the increase in population, and we want to keep the hoodlums off the church property," replied the speaker. "If we don't take adequate protective measures our members, especially some of the women, will not drive back in here to attend church meetings in the evening. We are suggesting that the parking lot be floodlighted if we can raise the money."

"How many new members do you believe we'll gain from the increase in the neighborhood population which you mentioned?" asked someone else.

"Very few," replied the chairman, "the strength and the future of St. Mark's rests on its present membership. Two thirds of the newcomers to this area will be living in public housing, and we doubt if many of them will be interested in our church. This is another reason why it is so very urgent that we go ahead with the program your trustees have recommended. The off-street parking is especially critical; last Sunday I counted the people coming to church and 93 per cent came by car. This four-part program is the best possible way to conserve the loyalty of our present members."

The story of St. Mark's illustrates the basic problem encountered in planning for the future of the church in urban renewal. This is a difference in perspective. Urban renewal is a multifaceted process, and the role of the church will be determined by the perspective of the participant in the renewal effort.

In the case of St. Mark's the chief city planner viewed the church as a neighborhood-oriented religious organization which could make a major contribution to an emerging sense of community. On the basis of this view the city prepared a plan which permitted the church to remain and enabled it to acquire additional land for development of a church program aimed at residents of the neighborhood.

The trustees at St. Mark's viewed urban renewal as an alien force which threatened the life and future of their church. They viewed their church as a member-oriented institution which gave first priority to maintaining and perpetuating its own life. Their different perspective caused the trustees to develop and recommend an action program which was out of harmony with the goals the planners had envisioned for St. Mark's.

Both reactions, that of the planners and that of the trustees, are typical and not at all surprising. Planners tend to be both institution-oriented and idealistic while trustees tend to be conservative and pragmatic. Both see the church and its reactions to urban renewal primarily in institutional terms.

This is appropriate, for urban renewal is concerned with the redevelopment of land, and the church is a land-using institution. During the first fifteen years of its life urban renewal resulted in the displacement not only of nearly 200,000 families, but also of an uncounted number of churches. A few of these congregations which were forced to move by urban renewal were unable to survive and faded from existence. Others moved to new locations, often closer to the homes of their members. Some remained at the old address, as did St. Mark's, and continued a ministry to their members regardless of place of residence. A few churches have been transformed by urban renewal, not just in terms of land and building, but rather in terms of mission and ministry. The differences in reactions reflect the differences in perspective.

If Protestants are to plan effectively for their church's role in the urban renewal process, it will be necessary for churchmen to look at urban renewal from at least four different points of view.

The Church as a Land User

The most obvious viewpoint is from the perspective of an institutional land user. This may also be the area where the problem of perspective is most crucial, for some churches find it difficult to distinguish between their interests and the public interest. It is hard for a local church to view itself and its role in the community objectively. Every denomination has local churches located in actual or proposed urban renewal areas. In many cases the local church property will be directly involved in the renewal process, probably more often in conservation or rehabilitation than in actual clearance. How will the church react to this? Will it regard urban renewal as a threat to the status quo or as an ally in the effort to renew society? Will the local church view urban renewal as the vehicle for escape from a hopeless situation or as the manifestation of God's creative power at work?

One of the nation's leading consultants in urban renewal recently told the author that he frequently has found local churches to be among the most adamant and emotional opponents of proposals to renovate the neighborhood in which the church is located. There have been other instances in which the local church yielded to the temptation to place possible monetary gains ahead of service. There have been several specific instances in which a denomination has sought to have the municipality buy its local church property even though there was no physical justification for clearing the church site. Urban renewal programs are not intended to provide profitable methods by which denominations can "close out" unwanted churches.

With the increasing emphasis on conservation and rehabilitation rather than on clearance, the local church may be challenged to take the lead in renovating its property and bringing it up to the new standard for its neighborhood. In many cases the congregation of the local church may not be able to finance this task. This may be a very severe problem in those neighborhoods where many of the church's members will be forced to rehabilitate their own homes or to move to new quarters as a result of the renewal program. Will the denomination stand ready to provide financial assistance to these local churches? Most or all the people living in some neighborhoods will be relocated. The church may be left with only a few members during most of the lengthy period required for the acquisition, clearance, sale, and redevelopment of the land. Will denominational leaders accept the responsibility for subsidizing the local church's operation during this interim period? If not what churches will be available to the people moving into the redevelopment area?

The church will be challenged to come up with new ideas for the efficient and effective use of its share of the land in a renewal area. The contemporary suburban idea of a sprawling plant with a large adjacent parking lot simply will not fit into most redevelopment proposals. The church as a land-using institution has a major responsibility to look at urban renewal from the perspective of stewardship of land. It must not, however, become so deeply involved in issues of land use that it fails to view urban renewal from other perspectives.

The Church as a Prophetic Voice

During the early 1960's it became fashionable for churchmen to denounce urban renewal as a bureaucratic monster which pushed Negroes out of their homes without providing adequate relocation housing. Others saw urban renewal as a device which used the machinery of local government to enrich private real estate interests.

Unfortunately there was considerable justification for these and similar criticisms, but these attacks by churchmen also revealed the lack of a positive theological interpretation of urban renewal. The basic concepts of urban renewal are consistent with the Christian gospel which emphasizes the importance of renewing influences on the world.

Instead of denouncing the whole idea of urban renewal, it would be far more appropriate for churchmen to develop an affirmative attitude toward the basic goals which are articulated in the Housing Act of 1949 and subsequent amendments.[1] When the practices of the local public agency, of the federal government, or of private redevelopers stray from the fulfillment of these goals the prophetic voice of the church should be heard.

When planners ignore the wants and needs of the residents of a neighborhood under consideration for renewal treatment the prophetic voice of the church should be heard.

When renewal officials abandon residential redevelopment for low- and middle-income families the prophetic voice of the church should be heard reminding everyone that this was the central goal of the original legislation.

When the residential redevelopment which has been undertaken reinforces and perpetuates segregated housing patterns the prophetic voice of the church should be heard.

When urban renewal projects are planned on the premise that Caucasians can move to the suburbs while Negroes must be "encouraged" to remain in the central city the prophetic voice of the church should be heard.

On these and similar subjects the voice of the church must be more than that of just another critic, it must be that of a

[1] Section 2 of the Housing Act of 1949 included these words. "The Congress hereby declares that the general welfare and security of the Nation . . . require . . . the realization as soon as feasible of the goal of a decent home and a suitable living environment for every American family. . . ."

constructive prophet. This will require a new and deeper involvement by churchmen in the renewal planning effort. It may require the church to support new tax levies, fair housing legislation proposals, extension of public housing, and similar proposals which are not always popular among individual church members.

In recent years churchmen have been tempted to relinquish urban renewal to the demonic forces of the world and to flee to the green pastures of suburbia. A more appropriate viewpoint would be to regard urban renewal as another channel through which the redeeming and renewing influence of God's love may be directed.

The Church as an Evangelist

Other agencies in society will be involved in urban renewal from the perspective of land-using institutions and critics, but only the church will also be involved as an evangelist. Too often in recent years the Protestant church has been overwhelmed by the need for new churches in booming suburban communities and has been unable to grasp the evangelistic possibilities of urban renewal. Too often the church has reacted to urban renewal as a land-using institution rather than as a *religious* institution.

During the first fifteen years of its life the current urban renewal program involved 1,500 projects in 750 cities in Title I projects. Two thirds of these cities had a population of less than 50,000. When completed these projects will provide new housing accommodations for more than 500,000 persons. By 1970 more than 2,000,000 Americans will be living in neighborhoods which have been subjected to extensive renewal treatment. If Protestant churches are to fulfill their evangelical responsibilities to these people careful planning will be required to answer the questions raised by urban renewal.

Frequently the high cost of acquiring and clearing slums results in intensive use of the redeveloped land. For example, a current project in downtown Cleveland, Ohio, involves the partial clearance of 165 acres of land. Currently the area includes about 1,000 permanent residents. The redevelopment plans call for 5,500 housing units—a population increase of 10,000 to 15,000 for this area! Similar changes have occurred or are in progress in New York, Philadelphia, Chicago, and other cities. Will the church be ready to come in during the early stages of reuse planning, long before anyone knows the religious preferences of the new residents, and offer to buy the land necessary to build a church in the redevelopment area? This must be a venture on faith, and the major financial burden will be on the denomination as a whole. There will be no congregation to carry even a part of the load until long after the decision has been made on whether or not the denomination wants to church the area. Often the decision will have to be made three or four years before the first residents move into their new homes. If the decision is in the negative, it means that denomination has closed the door on that particular area for many years.

This is indeed a major challenge. For many denominations it may mean a reversal of the recent tendency to move to the suburbs. In some instances a denomination will be faced with the question of moving back into a neighborhood it left only a few years earlier when the local church in that area decided to follow its members in their flight from the central city. Usually the cost of land and building will be substantially in excess of the price received by the local congregation when it sold out to a Negro congregation or a sect group. Criticism in such circumstances is inevitable, but inaction may be even more deplorable.

Another question will concern the area from which prospective members are to be drawn. Many residential renewal projects are but tiny islands in a large sea of blight. Will the new church seek to reach only the residents of the renewed area? Or will the church's outreach also include those who live in the nearby slums? Can the same church serve the residents of new deluxe apartments renting for seventy-five dollars per room and also the residents of the dilapidated structure that was a mansion in 1890 and today houses a dozen or more families from West Virginia or Mississippi?

Some may argue that the city is already overchurched and no new churches are needed. While this is true in many parts of urban (and rural) America, it is also true that in many cities the main-line Protestant denominations have largely abandoned the slums and do not possess any "rights" in the area that is to be developed. Unless Protestantism is alert it will be ignored in planning for the reuse of the cleared land. Contemporary renewal planning emphasizes the development of new neighborhoods that will include all the necessary community facilities for the residents of the redeveloped area. Are Protestant churches a necessary facility in such areas? Can the church evangelize and serve a brand new community with old churches located outside the renewal area?

The current emphasis on the conservation and preservation of older neighborhoods also offers the church a new evangelistic opportunity. This neighborhood renewal concept developed in recognition of the fact that in most blighted areas many of the buildings can be saved through constructive efforts. Cities cannot afford to completely write off whole neighborhoods. Several Protestant churches are now undertaking a similar approach to the people living in blighted neighborhoods. It is erroneous to "write off" these residents as people who cannot be served by main-line Protestantism. More and more we see that Protestant churches which had been ministering to members who long ago moved to suburbia are now focusing attention on the people living within the shadow of the church. These churches have discovered that within a few blocks of the sanctuary are thousands of persons who are in as great a need of spiritual renewal as their homes are in need of physical renewal. Rebuilding the physical neighborhood may be the responsibility of the government; helping the residents renew their lives is a proper task of the neighborhood church. Blight is at least in part a product of the hopelessness of the residents. Merely rehabilitating the structures will not eliminate this hopelessness. The evangelical church ministering to the people in its neighborhood may be able to serve Christ and fight blight at the same time by bringing to these people evidence of the redemptive love of God through Christ. This may be the greatest challenge confronting the church as it becomes involved in urban renewal planning.

The Church as a Minister

If Protestant churches are to be effective in planning for their role in urban renewal they must also see themselves as ministers. From this perspective they must be prepared to reexamine their ministry. Currently in many small and medium-size cities proposals are being discussed to rebuild substantial sections of the central business district. Should the old downtown church with an obsolete building on a postage-stamp size lot take this as a heaven-sent opportunity to rebuild on a five-acre lot on the outskirts of town? Is the church's purpose to minister to a particular group of people or to the people in a particular area? The answers will vary but the question is always relevant.

During the past two or three years there has been a marked revival of interest in "downtown" by a number of Protestant denominations. This new trend is still overshadowed by the enormity of the task of building new churches in suburbia, but it is a most significant development. Nearly every week one hears or reads of a congregation that voted to rebuild at or near its present central location rather than to move to the fringe of the urban area. Interestingly enough a large proportion of these decisions are occurring in cities of under 50,000 population. Likewise a significant number of new churches are being organized in "inner-city" situations. Urban renewal may facilitate this decision to broaden the church's ministry.

Churches that serve people living in areas proposed for renewal also are being confronted with a new challenge to their ministry. Many of these people have lived in the same house for decades; they know no other place. Talk about renewal, relocation, and redevelopment confuses rather than enlightens these folk who are not prepared to deal with a process that places a heavy emphasis on verbal skills. Some would rather die than start life over again in a strange neighborhood. A few do choose to die, either by their own hand or by surrendering the will to live. The situation often is further complicated by the relatively long period between the time rumors first begin to fly and the day the resident actually receives an eviction notice. Commonly this is two or three years, not infrequently it has been five or six years.

It is in this sea of uncertainty that the church is called to minister to a new kind of "displaced person." If he is able to relocate within the parish his church may offer him the only link he will have between the past and the future. It may also be the only agency that can help him accept the abrupt changes that go with urban renewal. The church also should be able to offer a theological explanation of the creative forces that may be a part of the renewal process. It may help him accept his own sacrifices in terms of a neighbor-centered concern for future generations of city dwellers. The universal church should be able to help him find a new church home if he is forced to seek a residence far from his old abode.

In addition to this church-centered type of counseling, the minister should be prepared to assist his parishioners in the other problems that often overwhelm residents who are suddenly confronted by the red tape of urban renewal. These problems include such varied and technical subjects as building code interpretation, relocation payments, rehabilitation programs, construction contracts, special assessments, and the negotiation of building loans. The minister may not be able to become an expert in each of these fields, but he should be acquainted with the agencies that are equipped to help the individual resident in these matters and be able to refer his people to the appropriate person or agency. Urban renewal is a very complicated process, and its effects are often most disruptive, not only on the landscape, but also on the private lives of the residents. The church may be the only agency to which they are willing to turn with confidence in times of distress and confusion. It should be prepared to provide help.

It is an unfortunate fact that the heaviest costs of urban renewal must be borne by the underprivileged, the down-trodden, the poor, and the weak. It is to these the church is called to minister. It is not a new call.

The effectiveness of Protestant planning for urban renewal will be greatly influenced by the ability of churchmen to stand back and view the entire renewal process from each of these four perspectives.

9

Lessons in Integration
+++

"THIS IS THE THIRD FAMILY TO MOVE IN SO FAR THIS MONTH."

"At this rate there soon won't be more than a half-dozen white families left in the neighborhood."

"Well, I guess we shouldn't object to their moving in here; they have to live somewhere. But I surely hate to think of how they'll soon be taking over our church."

"Yes, every Sunday when I walk into church I expect to find a bunch of them sitting waiting for the service to begin."

This conversation took place between an elderly widow and her neighbor as they sat in the neighbor's living room and looked through the lace curtains at what was taking place across the street. A rental truck was backed up to the front door, and a middle-aged Negro and a teen-age boy who might have been his son were carrying furniture from the truck into the house, which still had the "For Sale" sign stuck in the ground in the middle of the small patch of grass between the sidewalk and the house. The house was obviously at least forty years old, but it appeared to be in a good state of repair. No one came out of any of the neighboring houses to offer to help the two Negroes as they struggled with the furniture in the hot summer sun.

Will these and the other Negro newcomers flock to join the all-white Protestant chuches scattered through this neighborhood? Will they soon crowd out the white members who, with their parents and grandparents, built and maintained these lovely church buildings? Has experience taught us any lessons which might provide the answers to these questions?

While conditions do vary from one community to another, perhaps the most important observation is that Negroes are not going to rush into churches where they will not be welcome. This fact is substantiated by hundreds of experiences and yet is completely counter to the expectations of many white church people. This is evident in nearly any large-city neighborhood in which Negroes constitute the vast majority of the residents. Negroes can be seen in the stores, the theaters, the Y.M.C.A., the restaurants, the taverns, the bowling alleys, the lodge halls, and in nearly every other building. It is not uncommon, however, to discover one or two remaining Protestant churches with an all-white membership which have never had a Negro inside the building, except perhaps the janitor. Ask a member or the pastor if a Negro ever sought to gain admission, and the usual answer is, "No, except perhaps once or twice a Negro who was new in the neighborhood and thought this was a colored congregation."

Why have the Protestant churches been so slow to respond to the biblical imperative on this issue? Why has the one institution that has been most vocal in proclaiming the brotherhood of man under the Fatherhood of God been so slow in practicing what it preaches? An answer to these questions will provide a helpful background for understanding the lessons which have been learned by those congregations which have successfully responded to the challenge of integration. Before examining the apparent causes for the church's failure to integrate, two things should be said on behalf of the church. Most of the progress that has been made in advancing the cause of the Negro in America is directly attributable to the message in the Christian gospel. The abolition movement, the educational and vocational programs on behalf of the freedman following the Civil War, and the recent sit-ins and freedom rides were largely led by persons who felt compelled to take such actions because of their Christian convictions.

Furthermore, a great many Christian ministers have sincerely tried to encourage the growth of a congregational fellowship that ignored racial distinctions. Unfortunately and all too often, such efforts at integration resemble what occurred in a Protestant church in downtown Milwaukee. The minister and some of his laymen were attending a meeting at which the racial question was being discussed. This minister described the integration efforts of his church and pointed out that the membership roll included more than two dozen Negroes. When he had completed his remarks one of his Negro members said, "Yes, Pastor, you have accepted us into the membership of this church, but your people have not accepted us into the fellowship."

While a number of Protestant ministers have been reluctant to encourage integration, in the majority of cases the pastor has been much more willing to build an integrated congregation than has his white membership. The primary responsibility for the church's failure cannot be blamed on either its message or its ministry.

Lessons from Failure

One of the least understood causes for the failure of the integration effort is the difference of perspective. Thus far most white persons have failed to comprehend the Negro's point of view and have sought to integrate the Negro into the white man's church just as other efforts are being made to integrate the Negro into the secular world of the white man. Such a position completely ignores the growing desire of many Negroes to maintain a distinctive identity. If integration is thought of as a one-way street in which the Negro must become like his white counterpart in every respect except color of skin, then the effort is doomed to failure. The Negro church remains one of the few areas in which the Negro can retain his identity as an individual and yet have a vehicle for self-expression and the exercise of his own abilities. Not all Negroes want to become an indistinguishable part of a *white* society. Furthermore, there is no valid historical or biblical basis for the concept of Christianity as a white man's religion. Foreign missionaries have learned this lesson; now Americans must learn that this is also true in the United States.

Possibly the most significant reason for the church's lagging behind other segments of society on integration is that basically the local church is a private, voluntary association with almost complete power to determine its own course of action. In this respect it resembles other private institutions (lodges, fraternities, country clubs, et cetera) and these have been as slow, and often slower, to integrate than has the church. Like the private club, the church may become a captive of the past and the last place to which people turn in their resistance to the changes that are occurring all about them. By its very nature the private, voluntary association is largely immune to many of the forces making for change in the rest of society.

Most, but not all, of the great advances on the integration front have occurred where one of three coercive forces was present. The areas where the most has been accomplished include housing, employment (including sports and the military establishment), and the use of public accommodations. In each instance the coercive power of legal, economic, or political considerations has made it expedient for the decision makers to proceed with some degree of integration. The Protestant churches as private, voluntary associations appealing to the middle and upper economic levels of society are invulnerable to these sanctions.

A third important factor in delaying integration is the willingness of many churchmen to pay the high costs that often are involved in maintaining a segregated church. For example, in southwestern Akron one main-line Protestant church located in an excellent building on a main thoroughfare found that the neighborhood was rapidly becoming populated by Negroes. The congregation voted to sell its building for far less than its replacement value and to merge with another congregation of the same denomination which was housed in an inadequate frame building. The newly merged congregation has built a new church which is little improvement over the one abandoned in the Negro area.

A few blocks away another Protestant congregation, with an old frame building on an excellent site in a lovely residential neighborhood, decided to replace the old structure with a new 250,000-dollar plant at the same site. The first unit, a 75,000-dollar educational wing, was dedicated in 1955. Five years later the congregation decided to relocate and start building all over again. Negroes had begun to move into the neighborhood. Similar examples can be found in every large Northern city. As long as people are willing to pay the price the church can continue as a segregated institution—at least for a few more years. There is no permanent escape, but it is still possible to buy time if a congregation is willing to pay the price, and many are willing.

A fourth reason for the delay has been the failure of

churches to take a united position on the race issue. As long as some churches are willing to practice segregation it will be difficult for others to obey the biblical imperative. As long as some preachers will openly defend segregation as being compatible with the Christian message it will be difficult for other ministers to preach effectively a doctrine of universal love and brotherhood. As long as there is a church in the area where a white person can go on Sunday morning or Wednesday evening and be assured that a Negro will not come in and sit down beside him it will be difficult for other churches to abandon segregation.

This kind of "competition" is especially hard on the old neighborhood church which is composed largely of ex-residents who drive back into the area every Sunday morning. Rarely does such a beleaguered congregation feel sufficiently secure to undertake a crusade for integration when it is fighting for its very existence. Under such circumstances it is easy to say, "This is the right move to make, but not at this time. Right now we cannot afford to risk losing some of our old members or alienating the new ones. Later, perhaps."

These are among the principal reasons why so few Protestant churches are integrated. Some observers will protest that what appears to be the primary factor, segregated housing patterns, has been omitted. The disappearance of the geographical parish and the ability of most urban churches to draw people from a large area supports the contention that residential segregation is an excuse but not a reason for the perpetuation of racial segregation in Protestant churches.

Lessons of Success

Despite these obstacles a growing number of Protestant churches are responding creatively and positively to the integration issue. Most, but not all, of these churches are located in neighborhoods which once were inhabited only by white residents but which are now racially mixed. As was pointed out earlier the church often is the last institution in the neighborhood which the Negro newcomer will enter.

Negroes may militantly demand equal opportunities in employment, housing, and public accommodations, but rarely will they seek to enter a church which does not desire their participation. (The same applies equally to white people!) This obvious fact should dispel many myths and fears held by white church people who are afraid that when the first Negro moves into the neighborhood it means their church will soon become a predominantly colored congregation.

"Mark my words! If you adopt this resolution, every black man in the neighborhood will regard it as a personal invitation to him and his family. Within a year we'll be so crowded there won't be room for our own kids in Sunday school." Despite this warning the members of Christ Church voted forty-three to twenty-nine to add the words "Everyone welcome" to the bulletin board in the church's front yard.

What happened as a result? Experience indicates that putting up such a sign may result in one or two Negro families occasionally coming inside the building. But the suspicions engendered by two centuries of discrimination cannot be wiped out simply by putting a notice on the church's bulletin board. If the pastor undertakes an intensive door-to-door visitation effort he may persuade a couple of Negro families to attend. The congregation had expected and some had half feared that if they opened the doors Negroes would be flocking to the church in large numbers. Instead, despite their hard work the results have been limited.

Pastors who have gone through the experience suggest that it is not enough for a previously all-white congregation to open its doors and proclaim that everyone is welcome. They have to "prove" that they mean it and then be "approved" by members of the Negro community. This is an action-reaction process which requires the church to take the initiative and which is not completed until the Negro neighbors have evaluated the sincerity of the institution.

To a certain extent this same process takes place in all-white neighborhoods where there are major cultural, economic, and social differences between the members of the church and the residents of the neighborhood. It is a much more important factor, however, when racial distinctions are present. This is a result of the American system of no-reward racial segregation, which exhorts the Negro to show initiative but if he succeeds it denies him admission to the white man's clubs, churches, homes, and other symbols of equality. Thus when a white church deviates from this system it has to prove that it is sincere.

The process of gaining "approval" usually is rather slow and often is filled with disappointments. An example of this is the congregation which, soon after Negroes began to move into the neighborhood, decided to welcome everyone regardless of race. Finally, after several months of calling and other efforts which had yielded only nominal results, they decided to concentrate on the forthcoming daily vacation Bible school. Through posters and leaflets delivered to every home in the neighborhood, by calls and by word of mouth, they advertised their school as being open to "*every* neighborhood child." They had even been able to secure two Negro mothers as teachers. They planned for a total attendance of about a hundred youngsters.

On the first day only sixty were present, forty white children and twenty Negroes. By the second day word had been spread that Negroes really were welcome, and the number of colored children increased to sixty. On the third day there were forty white and seventy-five Negro children in attendance. The staff and leaders of the church were jubilant. They had finally been approved! With great enthusiasm they went ahead and planned the big program which would conclude the Bible school. This would be held in the church on a Friday evening. The children would present a program for their parents, and the evening would end with a worship service. Invitations were sent home with every child urging the parents to attend. The staff expected a total attendance, counting students, brothers, sisters, and parents, of well over 200, and they recognized that whites probably would constitute only a minority of the group. Less than one half of the Negro children and only seven Negro adults actually put in an appearance.

Naturally the staff and leaders were badly disappointed. In retrospect, however, it was clear what had happened. The church had been approved, but only for Negro children to attend vacation Bible school. It had yet to prove that it sincerely wanted adult Negroes to attend a program and worship service in the church at which adult white members also would be present.

Experience also indicates that a church in a racially changing neighborhood should avoid big, dramatic decisions in which the race issue overshadows the mission of the church. Demanding a congregational vote on whether the words "Everyone welcome" should be added to the bulletin board is not the way to move forward on the issue of integration.

Progress on most matters in society is made through a series of important small decisions. Thus it is wiser for a church *not* to call a special congregational meeting to vote on the issue of integration, but rather to have the commission on education decide whether there should be a special effort to enroll *all* interested neighborhood children in the vacation Bible school. It is wiser not to ask the congregation or church council to vote on the general question of accepting Negroes as members, but rather to let the commission on membership and evangelism decide on how they will conduct a neighborhood visitation program.

The pastor of one church which had successfully integrated summed up his experiences in these words: "In 1946 our church council voted it would not accept Negroes as members. This decision was never formally reversed, but today we have many Negro members. As we look backward we cannot point to any one date or decision and say, 'That was the turning point.' It has been a steady and gradual process in which a series of small decisions have added up to one major decision which in effect reversed the earlier action of the church council."

This is not a plea for gradualism but rather the suggestion that many unnecessary defeats can be avoided by not demanding more than is necessary at any one point in this process. This lesson is illustrated by an interview with the pastor of a United Presbyterian church which seven years ago was an all-white congregation. Today about 60 per cent of the members are Negroes, and the church is often referred to as one of the most successful examples of how integration can work.

This pastor was asked, "In looking back, what do you consider to be the single most important factor which helped your congregation successfully meet the challenge of integration?"

He smiled slowly and replied, "The guidance of the Holy Spirit."

"This I believe," was the response of the interviewer, "but what did you do that may have assisted the Holy Spirit?"

"Well, perhaps the most significant thing we did was made possible by our denomination's board of missions," he responded. "They provided the funds which enabled us to add a second staff person for three years. By having two full-time persons on the staff we were able to do three times as much pastoral calling as I had been able to do alone. Thus we were able to help all the members know everything that was happening, and the whole congregation moved along together on the road to integration. We were able to have many small groups meet together and discuss what was happening in the neighborhood and what it meant to each one of us and to Christ's church. The strong carried the weak. The emotionally secure members helped those who had been brought up in an environment where prejudice was the norm. Everyone had a chance to talk things through in a healthy atmosphere. Together we had the opportunity to grow in wisdom and, I hope, in grace."

This minister's remarks also illustrate another important lesson in integration: The necessity for dedicated pastoral care and internal communication in which each member, regardless of how active he may be, has the chance to talk through each issue as it arises.

The decision to integrate, however, is one which has repercussions beyond the individual local church.

Not long ago a young Negro couple attended the Sunday morning worship service of an all-white Lutheran church in an all-white upper-middle-class suburb. Everyone noticed the conspicuous strangers, and a couple of members introduced themselves and extended a word of welcome to the couple. No one thought much about the event. After all, one Sunday a few years earlier two Negro men had been in church. It turned out they were old college friends of the former pastor and were just passing through the city.

This time things turned out differently. After church the ushers sorted out the visitor cards from the offering plate and gave them to the chairman of the visitation committee, who passed them out to his helpers for follow-up telephone calls and visits. The following Tuesday evening his telephone rang, and when he picked up the receiver he heard, "Jack, this is Larry. Remember the Negro couple that was in church Sunday? Well, the first card you gave me to follow up on turned out to be that couple. Their name is Turner. They just moved here from Detroit, and while they live across the line in the city, they say this is the closest Lutheran church to their home, and they want to transfer their membership to this church. Get that, Jack? They want to transfer! They were members of a Lutheran church in Detroit and think they can transfer here. What are we going to do?"

Regardless of what Jack and Larry decide to do this episode illustrates another lesson that experience has taught about integration. If a local church decides not to admit Negroes into membership its action will tend to make many Negroes think that the entire denomination discriminates against the Negro. If one local congregation refuses to welcome a Negro into membership its action will make it difficult for other churches of that denomination elsewhere to evangelize among Negroes.

On the other hand, if a local church does welcome a Negro family into the life and fellowship of the congregation, that action has implications for other churches elsewhere. Someday one of these Negro families will move into a neighborhood near an all-white church of their denomination. As church members in good standing they have every right to expect to be able to transfer their membership. What will be the reaction of this congregation?

Both of these types of incidents have occurred and are occurring with increasing frequency. Their occurrence makes it clear that an effective program of racial integration cannot be carried on by one or two local churches; it must be a positive program which has the support of churches throughout the denomination.

Finally, there is real value in sharing experiences with

other churches which also are confronted with the question of integration. Obviously the church which has made the most progress can offer helpful advice and encouragement to the congregation which is only contemplating or just beginning integration. Such an interchange can be extremely helpful also to the members of the congregation who are asked to recount their experiences and advise. This helps them to structure their own thinking, to evaluate systematically their successes and failures, and to relate their individual experiences to the purpose and mission of the universal church. Such an interchange also helps the typical layman discover that his church and its problems are not unique, that he is a part of a larger interested and concerned fellowship, and that he has learned something which is of value to other churches.

These are some of the lessons which churches have learned from experience with integration. Will other churches be able to benefit from these experiences, or will they have to learn these same lessons the hard way?

10

The Church of Tomorrow
+++

THE PRIMARY FOCUS OF CHURCH PLANNING IS ON THE FUTURE.
This is in sharp contrast to much of the life of the church,
which both doctrinally and culturally is focused on the past.
This distinction is not absolute, however, for some of the
most important considerations in planning for the future of
Protestantism are events which occurred centuries ago. The
birth, life, death, and resurrection of Jesus; the origins and
development of the New Testament church; the letters of
Paul; and the teachings of Luther, Calvin, and other Re-
formers are historic events which are basic influences in planning for the church of tomorrow. There are many others.
There are also many secular forces at work in society today
which will influence the church of tomorrow.

One of the most common requests directed to the church
planner is that he should analyze these forces and trends and

forecast their impact on the church and the consequences of this impact. This is a request which is both tempting and legitimate. It also is fraught with risk. No one can pretend to predict with complete accuracy tomorrow's weather, much less the nature of tomorrow's church, but it is possible to distinguish some of the forces that have influenced the characteristics of today's church and to speculate on the impact that changes in these forces will have on the church of tomorrow.

From the perspective of a city planner turned clergyman, it appears that in many respects the church of tomorrow will resemble even more closely the society in which it exists than it does today. In several very significant ways, however, the church of tomorrow may bear a much greater resemblance to the New Testament church than does the church of today. Perhaps this can best be illustrated by first looking at the church from the "outside."

To those outside the Christian fellowship—and this probably includes millions of persons who have their names listed on the membership rolls of some local church—the church is seen most clearly in terms of the individual clergyman and the physical plant owned by the church. Thus any changes in the church of tomorrow may be most visible in these two areas.

Several trends already are apparent which suggest that the clergyman of tomorrow will differ from his counterpart of today and, more particularly, from the clergyman of yesterday. Foremost among these trends is the increasing emphasis on specialized training. The general practitioner is fast disappearing from the ranks of doctors, lawyers, engineers, teachers, physicists, chemists, and other professions. The age of specialization also is affecting preparation for the ministry. Most of the mainline Protestant denominations now require a college degree and seminary graduation for final ordination. In addition, many of the newer sects which until recently ridiculed the need for formal theological education are now developing their own colleges and seminaries.

In the church of tomorrow, however, the complex demands of the Christian ministry will require more than just a seminary degree. There will be greater emphasis on postgraduate training for the increasingly large number of clergymen who wish to specialize—in Christian education, pastoral counseling, preaching, church administration, youth work, and similar areas. This trend already is apparent in the first two fields mentioned. In the years to come it will apply with an even greater emphasis in education and counseling, and especially in administration at the denominational level. The day is fast approaching when the pastor who accepts the call to serve as synod president, district superintendent, archdeacon, or presbytery executive will be expected to embark on a serious in-service training program. Later on, a period of formal academic preparation probably will be required of many men who expect to serve in administrative and technical posts. This is not a criticism of nor any reflection on the men who have carried the administrative responsibilities of Protestantism. Rather it is a reflection of the increasing complexity of society. Perhaps the best example of this is the use of computers in operations research. The church cannot long ignore this movement which is revolutionizing administration in business, education, and government. On the other hand, only trained manpower will be able to utilize these new skills and techniques.

This same emphasis on training and skill will apply to other phases of the ministry. The pastor of a rural or small town congregation will be given the opportunity, and expected to take it, to "re-tool" before accepting a pastorate in a metropolitan situation. The minister who wants to serve in an inner-city situation or who wants to serve an unusually homogeneous congregation such as will be found in a "retirement village" or adjacent to a massive public housing project will have the opportunity for special preparation. Most ministers serving in parish situations will be encouraged to take specialized training in counseling.

Perhaps the second most important change in the role of the minister will be in how the pastor spends his time. Already most pastors are finding that an ever-increasing share of their workweek is devoted to counseling. This is a logical trend, for it reflects the deepening understanding of mental illness. This nationwide trend, which finds millions of laymen exhibiting an amazing degree of sophistication on the subject, means that doors are open for pastoral counseling which once were always closed. This does not necessarily indicate that people have more problems. It probably only means that they are now ready and often eager to talk about them with their pastor. The inhibitions of the past often meant that the preacher was the last person to know of an individual's personal problems; now the same person, or more likely his son or daughter, finds it easy to take his problems to the pastor. This change in attitude plus the great increase in church membership has resulted in a tremendous demand for pastoral counseling. It will be even greater in the church of tomorrow.

This increase in counseling and other specialized services combined with the greater affluence of most congregations and with other demands will increase the number and proportion of local churches with multiple staffs. This in turn will increase the pressure for specialization and formal postgraduate training. This increase in specialization will drastically alter the way many ministers spend their time. An increasingly large proportion of them will be devoting the bulk of their working time to one or two functions.

One of the possible fringe results of this increase in specialization may make the ministry once again an attractive vocation to large numbers of young men. The person who feels a
call to the ministry but cannot think of himself attending an
endless series of church meetings may see a place for himself
in one of the specialized ministries. The youngster who loves
people as individuals but is bored with group meetings may
specialize in pastoral counseling, while his opposite number
may specialize in the field of parish program administration.
The lad who is torn between a career in politics and a call to
the ministry may combine them by becoming a community
organizer or director of urban work for a denominational or
interdenominational group of churches.

While specialization will mean that the minister of tomorrow will concentrate most of his working day in one or two
functions, it also will require him to spend a substantial
amount of time "keeping up with his specialty." Some of this
will be in daily study, but much of it can come only from
periodic refresher courses in an academic atmosphere which
may run from a couple of weeks to several months in length.

Two other changes will influence the ministry of tomorrow's church. One is the already growing recognition that
in many situations the pastor cannot function effectively in
the isolation which is so typical of today's church. One answer to the problem of isolation is the group ministry. This
is an old concept with rural origins, but it may be the only
means to insure the psychological and spiritual survival of
the full-time Christian worker surrounded by a materialistic
culture. Today this concept is gaining wider acceptance for
those serving in the physically and religiously blighted sections of the inner city. Tomorrow it may spread to the suburban communities and include laymen as well as clergymen
as more and more people conclude they can get along without God and the church. The remaining minority may resur-

rect the New Testament concept of the church as a gathered community bound together by a spiritual, economic, and vocational discipline.

Closely related to this is the problem of the pastor's pastor. It has long been recognized that each pastor needs his own pastor. In the Roman Catholic Church this is clearly understood, and each priest has his pastor. In Protestantism the usual pattern has been for the bishop or for the regional executive (district superintendent, presbytery executive, synod president, et cetera) to serve as the pastor to the pastors within his jurisdiction. This was an acceptable system and frequently worked rather well. The decline of congregational autonomy and the increase in denominational centralization has adversely affected this structure, however. Frequently the pastor of a local church feels his regional executive is so burdened with administrative responsibilities that it would be an intrusion to bother him with personal problems. Equally significant is the shift in the power structure. More and more pastors are realizing that their future rests in the hands of this regional executive, who often determines pastoral appointments and screens congregational requests for new ministers. Can they risk taking their problems to the man who also controls their career? Perhaps the responsibilities of administrator and of pastor no longer can be delegated to the same person. Thus it would appear that in the church of tomorrow a new single-function post, pastor to pastors, will emerge. (This is another example of the specialization referred to earlier.) Whether this will be structured on a local interdenominational level or on a denominational basis covering a larger geographical area probably will be determined by local circumstances.

The other area in which outsiders may find the church of tomorrow to be quite different from today is in the nature and importance of the church's physical plant. Today outsiders and insiders both tend to overemphasize the importance of the church building. If a suitable replacement can be found for the building as the status symbol of a congregation, then important progress can be made in the life and mission of the church.

Already certain advances have been achieved. There is a growing acceptance, usually resulting more from economic than aesthetic or symbolic considerations, that a new church does not have to "look like a church." This is far from a concensus, and many congregations are still copying thirteenth- or eighteenth-century architecture, often with unfortunate results in terms of both function and form. Hopefully the church of tomorrow will be designed for the specific needs of the people living in its vicinity rather than as a nostalgic link with the past. This will be most readily apparent in the new congregations which will be found in the inner city, in urban redevelopment areas, and in high density apartment neighborhoods. Function and economy will be the dominant forces. Some congregations may elect not to have any building, meeting instead in homes. In others most of the ministry of the church will be offered in the homes, the offices, the streets, and the stores, not in a special building.

There will be an effort, but only partially successful, to reverse one of the church planning principles discussed in Chapter 5 and to have the needs of the people, not the physical nature of the building, determine the content of the program and how the minister spends his time.

In the same vein the church of tomorrow will take a new approach to Christian education. It is beyond the scope of this book to predict what this will be, but it is now clearly understood that transmission of the gospel involves more than construction of a large new educational wing. Perhaps tomorrow the church will spend its money on training parents to be teachers rather than on erecting buildings. Perhaps the religious education plants constructed during the past few years will be used as Protestant parochial schools. Perhaps a "released" or "shared" time arrangement with the public schools will be widely used. Perhaps the current trend toward weekday sessions of the church school will increase with an even greater emphasis on fellowship, nurture, and instruction—and time for all three. The congestion of the peak-hour Sunday morning schedule combined with the high hourly costs of contemporary church buildings may force the church of tomorrow to move away from Sunday school and toward Christian education.

One of the basic assumptions in this attempt at prophecy is that the greatest changes that have occurred in the outward form of the church during recent years have been caused by secular forces and that this will continue to be true in the foreseeable future.

This can be seen by reviewing recent American history. The impact of the conflict over Negro slavery, the decline of the rural farm population, the Supreme Court's decision banning segregation in public schools, the suburbanization of the urban population, and the contemporary efforts to renew the central core of our great cities have had profound effects on the policies and forms of the Protestant churches in America. What are the similar secular trends and forces that will influence the church of tomorrow?

Perhaps the most crucial social problem confronting Protestantism today is in the field of race relations. Today the church is one of the last holdouts in a society that is gradually but surely shifting from a segregated to an integrated form. The continued migration of Southern Protestants, both white and Negro, to Northern cities will hamper efforts to increase the number of integrated local churches. An even stronger counterforce will be the relaxation of racial restrictions in the housing and employment fields. As more and more whites and Negroes are able to mix both at home and at work it will become easier for Protestant churchmen to accept the idea of an integrated Christian fellowship. This will be far from a universal condition, however. In many communities the Protestant churches, the private clubs, the swimming pools, and the third-rate eating places are the only "public" places left in which a policy of racial segregation can be maintained. Legal and social sanctions may remove the last three from this list. Tomorrow may find the Protestant churches the last segregated institutions in many communities. For many persons it will continue to be the one place left to which they may go with confidence that Negroes will not come in and sit down beside them.

Closely related to the issue of race relations in America is the rise of nationalism abroad, particularly in the underdeveloped areas of the world. This already has had a definite effect on the whole approach to the missionary program of the church. Obviously this will result in a new role for the missionary of tomorrow. It appears inevitable that the leadership in the missionary movement of tomorrow will be drawn, not from "foreigners," but from indigenous sources. This probably will apply to both local and international positions. This trend is already quite apparent—it merely remains to be accepted as the only possible effective alternative—and it will be accepted in the church of tomorrow.

When it is accepted it will have far-reaching effects on the entire church, for it will radically change the approach of American Protestantism to foreign missions. Two examples will illustrate this contention. First of all, it will require a completely different approach and attitude by denominational boards of foreign missions. Today they are geared to recruit and service a small army of dedicated Americans serving overseas. Tomorrow their task will be quite different. It will resemble the Point Four program of the United States during the 1950's or the present program of many boards of American missions. Instead of supporting people in the field the board of foreign missions will become an agency offering advice, expertise, and aid to local chuches around the world. Instead of sending people out for five-year terms to do a job they will send a consultant out for five days to advise the local leaders who are the doers. The board will become church-centered rather than person-centered in its operation.

A second example of the impact of this change will be on the local church which has been stimulated to support foreign mission work through identification with an individual serving in the foreign field. In the church of tomorrow money will have to be raised if the gospel is to be preached and the sacraments administered in all the nations of the world. What will replace the contemporary identification with an American missionary? Will the local church "adopt" a congregation in another nation? Will a churches-to-churches program paralleling the "sister cities" idea that originated in 1958 be developed? Or will churchmen simply be asked to give out of a sense of the Christian imperative?

Ever since December 4, 1960, when Eugene Carson Blake preached his historic sermon on the reunion of Protestantism, the topic of denominational mergers has been one of the most discussed subjects in the church. If one accepts the thesis that the church is greatly influenced by secular forces there are three reasons for anticipating major progress in the efforts toward church unity. The first is that the contemporary climate is pro-merger. Whether one looks at school districts, grocery chains, airlines, hotels, industrial firms, or the various branches of Lutheranism, one finds a pronounced acceptance of the values of merger. The more frequently mergers occur in the secular world the easier it will be for churchmen to accept the personal sacrifices that may be involved. The contemporary "urge to merge" almost certainly will have a pronounced effect on the form of tomorrow's church.

The second secular force is the growth of the so-called "American religion" which tends to gloss over denominational differences and which has resulted in tremendous support among laymen for organic merger of Protestant denominations. Disciples of this American religion see no differences between Presbyterians and Congregationalists, between Episcopalians and Methodists, or between Baptists and Disciples. This has resulted in important pressures on pastors and denominational leaders to forget their differences in polity, liturgy, theology, and traditions and come together in the cause of unity. While a theological defense can be made for such an argument, much of the present pressure appears to be derived from secular rather than religious forces.

The third secular factor is the cult of efficiency and economy, which long has been used as an argument for church merger at both local church and denominational levels. While this has obvious applicability to the two or three very small congregations in the small town, each with their own building and pastor, it is of doubtful validity when applied to the merger of large institutions such as business corporations, units of government, or denominations. Experience indicates that the proportionate cost of overhead for staff, et cetera, rises with an increase in size.

Countering these secular forces which favor merger is the recent resurgence in denominationalism which now appears to be in only the beginning stages of a long-range trend. The stronger the denominational ties, the more difficult is organic merger. It is true that a well-organized denomination with a strong centralized place of authority is better equipped to implement a merger decision than is a denomination which is in fact a very loosely organized confederation of local churches. This same centralized strength also has built into it, however, many elements which are most comfortable when the status quo is not threatened as it would be by mergers. It would appear that the growing sense of denominationalism will tend to slow merger proposals in the church of tomorrow.

This rise of denominationalism can be seen most clearly in the field of church polity. It now appears that the future is almost certain to witness a further deterioration of congregational autonomy. The American Baptist Convention and several Lutheran groups already have expressed a deep concern over the dangers and disadvantages that appear to be inherent in this form of church polity. In addition, as Protestantism continues increasingly to resemble secular institutions in such areas as administration, finance, personnel administration, planning, and promotion, it appears inevitable that the centralizing forces that have affected these secular institutions will also prevail in the church. Perhaps even more influential will be the sheer facts of life. For example, the increasing shortage of trained clergymen makes it more difficult for a local church to call a pastor without any professional assistance. The demand for an educated clergy will force the denominations to be more active in the area of higher education. The inevitable vocational specialization of the clergy discussed earlier will require the denomination to operate not only seminaries for the preparation of young ministers, but also in-service training facilities for pastors who have been out of school for several years. The same emphasis on specialization will make it very important that the local church be served by a pastor with the appropriate training and experience. Seldom will a local pulpit committee be as well equipped to appraise objectively its own needs and the qualifications of potential candidates as is the trained denominational official charged with ministerial placement.

The almost universal acceptance of the funded pension system involves a strengthening of the denomination at the expense of the local church. The typical pastor is becoming increasingly dependent on his denomination for his training, his employment, his pension, his professional fellowship, his opportunities for advancement, and his chances for greater self-expression and status through service on boards and committees. This change is reducing the autonomy of the local congregation. As the minister becomes an organization man and the denomination becomes *the* organization the role of the local church diminishes. Instead of being *the organization,* it becomes a part of the larger organization and thus loses some of its independence. The high cost of organizing a new suburban congregation and subsidizing it during its formative years means a shift away from the "mother church" concept and toward better-financed denominational home missions agencies. Perhaps most important of all, the frequent lack of concern by a congregation for the people in the immediate neighborhood of the local church, best illustrated by the many congregational decisions either to move from the central city to the suburbs or to remain in the inner city but to serve an absentee congregation, has demonstrated the need for a stronger denominational voice if the mission to the inner city is to be fulfilled. In an urban renewal situation it usually is completely beyond the financial capabilities of any one congregation to acquire the site and build an appropriate structure. A re-entry into a slum area also requires the kind of investment in money and manpower that apparently can be supplied only by a central denominational agency. Likewise, if the church is to be an effective force in the total life of the world it must speak with fewer but more persuasive voices.

This inevitable decline of congregational autonomy and the accompanying centralization of the decision-making process within the hierarchy of the denomination is not necessarily a deplorable trend. While it is true that power does have a corrupting influence, it is also true that independence has encouraged irresponsibility. Furthermore each local church does have a Christian interest in the concerns of other Christians and other churches. A decrease in congregational autonomy may enable the denomination to be the channel through which this concern is transmitted and implemented. If this does happen the brotherhood of man under the Fatherhood of God will be more apparent in the church of tomorrow than it is in the church of today.

Perhaps the most difficult challenge to the future of the Protestant churches may come in the competition for the leisure time of the individual. As the real workweek continues to decrease the competition rapidly increases for the free time and uncommitted money of the individual. In the past a person's job was the principal factor in determining how much time he had available for church activities. Recently, as leisure time has increased, many churches have sought to compete by organizing bowling leagues, baseball teams, lecture series, and other secular forms of free-time activity. (This is not intended as a condemnation of all such groups. Occasionally such activities have made a unique Christian contribution to the life of the total community. For example, in one suburban church the economic power of the church bowling league was used to end the traditional pattern of racial segregation in local bowling establishments.)

In the future this competition will become more sophisticated and more intense. It is unlikely that more than a few churches will be able to maintain extensive and varied leisure-time programs. Already a trend away from this pattern is apparent. It centers around the development of small Bible-study fellowship groups. While still a very small movement, this trend has greatly impressed many serious observers of the state of the church. Quite possibly the church of tomorrow may be sponsoring more Bible-study groups and fewer bowling teams as it specializes in those areas of leisure-time activities in which it has a unique contribution to offer.

A second trend, still largely in the conversation stage, which may have a profound effect on the laity is the proposal that in each metropolitan area there be established a lay training school which would provide formal training for laymen. The courses would be equivalent in length, sophistication, and content to those taught on the college or seminary level but would be aimed to reach the housewife whose children are grown, the active layman who regrets his lack of formal training in Christianity, and the retired person, old in years but young in body and spirit, who would like to offer a large bloc of time to his church in a semiprofessional role. Some of these may be interdenominational lay academies; others will be operated by a single local church or denomination with a strong denominational orientation. Whatever form they take they will represent a marked improvement over the current ten or twelve hour courses that are intended to educate the man in the pew.

The central theme in any discussion of the church of tomorrow is the importance and influence of change. This means that an unchanging gospel must be presented to people living in a rapidly changing world. Within this context of change the church of tomorrow must be able to adopt and adapt improvements in its means of communicating without altering the message. In the church of tomorrow as in the church of yesterday and today the central purpose of the church will be to communicate the truth and the implications of the life, death, and resurrection of our Lord and Savior.

Selected Bibliography

++++++++

Beaver, R. Pierce. *Ecumenical Beginnings in Protestant World Mission.* New York: Thomas Nelson & Sons, 1962.

Berdyaev, Nicholas. *The Destiny of Man.* New York: Charles Scribner's Sons, 1937.

Breese, Gerald, and Whiteman, Dorothy E., editors. *Approach to Urban Planning.* Princeton, N.J.: Princeton University Press, 1953.

Carroll, Charles E. *The Community Survey in Relation to Church Efficiency.* New York: The Abingdon Press, 1915.

Cox, David F., and Devine, Michael T. "Urban Church Location," *Church Management* (October, 1962).

Dahl, Robert A. *Who Governs?* New Haven, Conn.: Yale University Press, 1961.

Davis, James H. *The Outsider and the Urban Church.* Philadelphia: Board of Missions of The Methodist Church, 1962.

Douglass, H. Paul. *Church Comity.* New York: Institute of Social and Religious Research, 1929.

Duhl, Leonard J., editor. *The Urban Condition.* New York: Basic Books, Inc., 1963.

Everett, Robinson O., editor. "Urban Renewal," *Law and Contemporary Problems.* Durham, N. C.: Duke University School of Law (Autumn, 1960; Winter, 1961).

Fichter, Joseph H. *Social Relations in the Urban Parish.* Chicago: University of Chicago Press, 1954.

Geen, Elizabeth, *et al.*, editors. *Man and the Modern City.* Pittsburgh: University of Pittsburgh Press, 1963.

Goodman, Paul, and Goodman, Percival. *Communitas.* New York: Vintage Books, 1960.

Guild, Roy B., editor. *The Manual of Interchurch Work.* New York: The Federal Council of Churches of Christ in America, 1917.

Ham, Clifford C. "How Does the Planning Process Operate?" *The City Church* (May-June, 1961).

Handy, Robert T. *We Witness Together.* New York: Friendship Press, 1956.

Hiltner, Seward. "Planning as a Profession," *Journal of the American Institute of Planners.* Vol. 23, No. 4.

Hoover, Robert C., and Perry, Everett C. *Church and City Planning.* New York: Dept. of the Urban Church, National Council of Churches in Christ, 1955.

Howes, Robert G. *The Church and the Change.* Boston: Daughters of St. Paul, 1961.

Jacobs, Jane. *The Death and Life of Great American Cities.* New York: Random House, Inc., 1961.

Kloetzli, Walter. *The Church and the Urban Challenge.* Philadelphia: Fortress Press, 1961.

Kloetzli, Walter, and Hillman, Arthur. *Urban Church Planning.* Philadelphia: Fortress Press, 1958.

Kolko, Gabriel. *Wealth and Power in America.* New York: Frederick A. Praeger, Publisher, 1962.

Lasswell, Harold D., and Kaplan, Abraham. *Power and Society.* New Haven, Conn.: Yale University Press, 1950.

Lee, James M. "The Role of the Planner in the Present," *The Journal of the American Institute of Planners,* Vol. 24, No. 3.

Lee, Robert, editor. *Cities and Churches.* Philadelphia: The Westminster Press, 1962.

———. *The Social Sources of Church Unity.* Nashville: Abingdon Press, 1960.

Leiffer, Murray H. *The Effective City Church.* 2nd rev. ed.; Nashville: Abingdon Press, 1961.

MacFarland, Charles S. *Christian Unity in Practice and Prophecy.* New York: The MacMillan Company, 1933.

Marty, Martin E. *Second Chance for American Protestants.* New York: Harper & Row, Publishers, 1963.

Millett, John D. *The Process and Organization of Government Planning.* New York: Columbia University Press, 1947.

Musselman, G. Paul. *The Church on the Urban Frontier.* New York: Seabury Press, 1960.

Norton, Perry L., editor. *Search*. New York: National Council of the Churches of Christ in the U. S. A., 1960.

Perloff, Harvey S., editor. *Planning and the Urban Community*. Pittsburgh: University of Pittsburgh Press, 1961.

Pratt, William David. "The Church in City Planning," *The City Church* (March-April, 1959).

Ramage, David. "The Congregation as an Instrument of Change," *The City Church* (November-December, 1963).

Sanderson, Ross W. *The Church Serves the Changing City*. New York: Harper & Brothers, 1955.

Schaller, Lyle E. *The Challenge of Urban Renewal*. Philadelphia: Board of Missions of The Methodist Church, 1961.

———. "Planning: Product or Process?" *Mayor and Manager* (December, 1963).

———. *Resources for Local Church Planning*. Philadelphia: Board of Missions of The Methodist Church, 1962.

———. "What Is an Asset?" *The City Church* (March-April, 1964).

Shippey, Frederick A. *Church Work in the City*. Nashville: Abingdon Press, 1952.

Smith, Philip M. "Protestant Comity in Metropolitan Pittsburgh," *American Sociological Review*, Vol. 8, pp. 425-32.

Soth, Lauren K. "Farm Policy for the Sixties," *Goals for Americans*. Englewood Cliffs, N. J.: Prentice-Hall, Inc., 1960.

Temple, William. *Nature, Man and God*. London: Macmillan & Company, Ltd., 1934.

Walker, Robert A. *The Planning Function in Urban Government*. Chicago: University of Chicago Press, 1950.

Wilson, Robert L. *An Example of Local Church Planning*. Philadelphia: Board of Missions of The Methodist Church, 1962.

———. *Questions City Churches Must Answer*. Philadelphia: Board of Missions of The Methodist Church, 1962.

Wilson, Robert L., and Waltz, Alan K. *The Methodist Church in Urban America*. Philadelphia: Board of Missions of The Methodist Church, 1962.

Winter, Gibson. *The New Creation as Metropolis*. New York: The Macmillan Company, 1963.

———. *The Suburban Captivity of the Churches*. Garden City, N. Y.: Doubleday & Company, Inc., 1961.

Index

+++++

219

Date